To Father Russell, who is "real cool".

Grace,
The Gateway,
In the Era of the
Secular

by Fr. Dale Tupper

*Enjoy!
Katherine & George F.*

Table of Contents

1. Writing as Prayer

- Therefore, since we have a great high priest who has passed through the heavens, Jesus, the Son of God, let us hold fast to our confession. For we do not have a high priest who is unable to sympathize with our weaknesses, but one who has similarly been tested in every way, yet without sin. So let us confidently approach the throne of grace to receive mercy and to find grace for timely help.
Hebrews 4:14–16

Catholics in a Climate of Hostility

The issue before us today is the challenge of being a Catholic in an upended and twisted time. Clearly, this culture in the United States is hostile in many ways to whatever is Catholic. Our entire values system as Catholic is considered an affront to whatever this culture would seek to become. That hostility is becoming palpable in the events of this postmodern world.

Our consent and submission is more and more being asked. It is not enough to consent that these cultural changes be allowed today. The liberal movement of these times expects Catholic participation as a kind of loyalty test. Assent and participation are close to being required of every Catholic, even if it contradicts the Word of God in our times.

In many ways, we are still off guard regarding the challenges of these times. I suspect that, had we been watching carefully, we would have seen these times approaching us, and might have responded more quickly and more directly. Yet here these times are, and we need to address how we are to live in the midst of such a fragmenting and chaotic context, a time in contradiction to the call of the Gospel.

I had read recently that in the Communist countries of Eastern Europe freedom of religion meant only the right to attend church. Everything else belonged to the state. Nothing else but that one freedom was allowed, just to attend worship. This comes very close to what many here redefine freedom of religion to be, only a freedom to attend worship.

Obviously, what many have had in mind was that the rest of religion was no longer a right. Morality then had to dovetail with whatever the supreme court would decree, or whatever dogmas identity politics would proclaim. Any other freedom of religion now is expected to belong to the government. As a result, anyone who truly owns their Catholic faith has found themselves more and more isolated in this supposedly liberal democracy that is anti-Christian to the max.

This has been a surprising turn of events, a blatant attempt to redefine both the limits of our faith, as well as the extension of the power of this secular era. We should not misread these events.

The Paper Tiger Illusion

I had intended to retire, and to live out my days in a kind of quiet and comfort. On one day of prayer, however, I found myself at a new threshold, a kind of potential for something I had never before planned to do.

I found myself thinking that the Lord might like me to put into words some of the quandary in which Catholics find themselves in this 21st Century. I thought that we need to ground ourselves better in hope and expectation for the conclusion to which the cross is pointing.

I doubt that there has been a time like the one that we are living in today, at least one so universal in its consequences. As we reach back over two thousand years of Christianity we can quickly recognize that something has changed in this 21st Century in a massive way. Furthermore, the change is not ours, but the realm in which we live. Something is wildly out of focus regarding to what and where this world is tending.

In this new context, at times we wonder if it is ourselves that have lost our way. In fact, it is not we who are lost. It is instead this brave new world that is lost in these times. This context is both a challenge and an opportunity. My hope is that the mystery of grace in our faith might be a source of assistance for both the challenge to us as Catholics, as well as an opportunity for all who might seek Christ, but have not yet found Him.

Despite the pointedness of my words, I am less interested in how these times might confront us. The enemies of true faith should not be the focus of our energies.

I am much more interested in addressing the unique and transcending gifts of the Gospel in our daily lives. These times are a paper tiger in the face of Jesus Christ. Satan's message is to suggest that we are sinking into a kind of irrelevancy as disciples of Christ. This secular message is that there is no hope for our Catholic way of living. Nothing could be further from the actual truth.

To write about the mysteries of faith that surround us is a form of prayer for me. I find the experience of writing today an opportunity to reflect in prayer about these things that our faith should be thinking about in this era. Perhaps the words of 1st Peter 2:23 might be appropriate here:

- "You have been born anew, not from perishable but from imperishable seed, through the living and abiding word of God."

My constant hope is that anything that I write will give glory and honor to the Lord.

Saint Therese

Some years back I had heard a presentation about Saint Therese, the Little Flower, that when she was dying, she pledged herself to work in eternity to bring about conversion and redemption for the good of this world. I thought that her perspective was unique, that most at the point of death would be looking forward to the rewards and blessings of the afterlife. She was not.

Here was Therese asking the Lord to let her labor for the good of souls in eternity. No doubt, this commitment was part of what went into making her a saint for our times. It is also part of what has made her the patron of the missions and a doctor of the church. This was an astounding development for someone who never left the French convent where she had lived, from the age of thirteen until her death in her mid twenties. Who would have imagined that such a cloistered and isolated young woman would become the patron of the missions in this world, and a doctor of the church.

I know it is somewhat naive on my part, but I had thought that her chosen mission would be a wonderful part of eternal life, directing ourselves back to this world in these last days. I ask the Lord to let me help in this regard for our times and the souls of this world, still caught in the uncertainties and confusions of this era of the secular.

Only after I began to write seriously about the mysteries of our faith for these times did I stop to wonder if this is how my original prayer might be answered. Perhaps is some way, what I write might become a resource, a point of reflection for those who are trying to take their faith seriously in these secular times, or for even those in search of a faith for these times. Even if there was only just a secret effort to write something for the Lord, I hope this action alone would still somehow be a witness to the Gospel. To compose these essays would be enough.

I think I should not waste this opportunity from the Lord. This is my prayer. Just the opportunity to address these times would be a kind of prayer for our times. That truly would be my only hope for any of this writing. Perhaps, if there is any merit in what I write, the Lord would use it to serve somehow in these last days, in the final victory of the cross of Christ over this world.

I would hope that the Lord would use this effort in whatever way to serve the good of the Church in these days of the 21st Century. I am satisfied either way. Just writing is my prayer to Christ, and that alone is enough for me. For me, writing itself is a joy.

The Subject of This Book

The subject of grace is what I'd like to talk with you about in these essays. As a topic, grace is often a little hard to grasp, something a little like gravity, a force that we can sense, but not a thing we can picture. We have trouble getting our arms around the grace that is present in our lives. Grace is the engine of the spiritual life, something of the divine that we can sense when in its presence, but nothing that we can just possess, or contain, because it always comes from above.

Yet grace is the essence of what so changes us from creatures trapped in the fallen state of original sin into the children of God. Grace at its simplest, and most profound, is the love of God for us, a love that reaches back into eternity, beyond our creation. This grace also reaches to the other end of time, all the way to the final climax of all existence.

Grace is the love that sent the Son into our world to provide a completion for our redemption by virtue of the cross. Grace, we know, arises from within the Trinity, from the love between the Father and the Son that showers the Holy Spirit on our world. Grace is what lifts us up into a state of supernature, the new life of the Gospel, to become the new creation of which Saint Paul writes.

Counterpoint to Grace

Beyond just the topic of grace, there is this bizarre context of the 21st Century in which we live, this postmodern world, apparently graceless. This era remains convinced that there is no such thing as the grace that we, as Catholics, know inundates our existence. Here in this 21st Century, never to this extent, have two such contradictory things governed daily living, divine grace versus the empty, material secularism of our times.

Each is the antithesis of the other, with absolutely no common ground, with an abyss between them. Without a clear and strong sense of the grace that infuses our lives, Catholics are blindsided by the extremity of the secular that exists today. This era is subtly pulled into a delusional form of existence where nothing can be defined, not truth or goodness, purpose or identity, meaning or value.

Thus the need for us as Catholic to identify the very nature and heart of grace within us. We need to recognize what divine grace does to and for us. We need to thoroughly sense how this grace lifts us up to a form of identity and meaning that exceeds even our very nature. In short, every Catholic today needs to have a solid grasp of the gift of grace that has come to us from above. Grace, in fact, is the gateway of eternal life in this world. Grace redefines our presence in these times. Grace will define us forever.

Join me, on this little foray into the topic of grace within this era of the secular.

2. The Difference

- For God so loved the world that he gave
  his only Son, so that everyone who believes in him might not perish but might
  have eternal life. For God did not send his
  Son into the world to condemn the world,
  but that the world might be saved through
  him. Whoever believes in him will not be
  condemned, but whoever does not believe
  has already been condemned, because he
  has not believed in the name of the only
  Son of God.
  John 3:16-18

The Unique Times in Which We Live

There is something intrinsically different about
this era, the one in which we are living — the 21st
Century in America. This era differentiates us
from every previous era. This something can't be
identified by the technology in which we live, the
apparent wealth of the Western world, or even the
existence of the internet and the electronic, digital
environment of these times.

Not that these things are not significant, they are.
However, to think that these elements of contemporary life are the essence of what is different

massively underestimates what is unique to existence here in this era, in these decades of the 21st Century.

Conversions in Asia

I've had the experience, a couple of different times, to taste the eras of the past, by experiencing cultures that had not yet redefined themselves in the climate of the 21st Century that we here in America are experiencing now.

One such experience was my five years as a Maryknoll associate missioner to the Republic of South Korea. It was the 1980's, the last remnants of the missionary church there. It was a church rapidly coming into its own, after decades, possibly after centuries of persecution, poverty, starvation, and invasions. What I saw there in those five years were times of significant evangelization.

There was a miraculous growth of Catholicism there, almost similar to the time of the Acts of the Apostles. That culture had a kind of theological awareness unlike anything I had experienced in the U.S. For centuries in Korea there had been an awareness that there was some divine being over everything. However, that divine being had always been just beyond their reach, inaccessible for their 5000 year history.

It was presented to me that the culture had perceived an abyss between themselves and this divine being, that there was no way to make contact with whomever and whatever this divinity might consist of. There was virtually no way, no dialogue connecting the culture to that undefined divinity.

Instead the culture was hammered by spirits, a kind of Shamanism where the spirits had control, and were petty dictators of the realm of sickness and knowledge, of bad luck and unforeseen catastrophe. The culture could sense that they were victims of someone spiritual, someone often filled with a kind of jealousy and envy. Seances and magic were used to bargain with that spirit world, and to try to give its people some hope of survival or prosperity.

These spirits were often seen to be more petty than malicious, but could easily become angry. The spirits were in control. Luck could be swayed by contact with those spirits. Newborn children were given a false name for the first 100 days, so that the spirits would not be jealous and send illness and death to the newborn. All kinds of fortune tellers were present even into the 1980's. Divination, tarot cards, the four pillars of your date of birth, all were used to try to predict the future, to ward off bad luck, to give guidance as to whom you should or should not marry.

Even in the midst of high rise construction in Seoul, often a major step of construction was to set up totems in the entrance to protect the workers and the building into the future. Villages in the countryside had totems at their gates, symbolic figures to ward off evil spirits. Buddhist monasteries sought to drive away bad spirits, and to call good spirits at their prayer times.

Loyalty to the spirits was expected. Shamanists were called up regularly to ferret out guidance and protection for individuals and families. In all of this, there was a kind of spiritual slavery to this spirit world that was the cost of protection.

The Coming of Christ into This Context

It was into this context that faith in Jesus Christ arose, first of all, from the Catholics of southern Japan, originally converted there by Saint Francis Xavier in the 1550's, and secondly, by books and catechisms brought to Korea, written by Fr. Matteo Ricci, a Jesuit missioner to China, around the early 1600's.

Given the Shamanistic climate, the Gospel took root with ease among many, but quickly resulted in persecution. The heart of the message to those who first discovered Catholicism was that, by turning your life over the Jesus Christ, you no longer were under the power of that spirit world, no longer a slave to their lies. No longer did you need to try to control the future, because your future was in God's hands, and God was a God of love. No longer was God distant, but in the Mass and Eucharist Christ could live in the heart and soul of each and every catholic, because Christ had defeated the power of the spirit world through the wood of the Cross. No longer did they need to attend seances or give money to the shaman.

This Christo-centric discovery was enough to bring about tens of thousands of converts and thousands of martyrs for the faith over the past 200 years. I understand that there are still many converts coming, right up into the 21st Century.

The heart of the matter in this story is that Catholicism in Korea grew up in an awareness about God, formerly distant, and about the spirit world of Satan. Before the missioners arrived, the Holy Spirit had already prepared the hearts of the people of that culture. When the missioners arrived, many immediately took to the good news of the Gospel. It was a two century long "Acts of the Apostles."

Catholicism in this Hemisphere

One more story of the past. Another culture found a similar kind of theological awareness.

One of the opportunities that I had as a pastor in Southern Minnesota was to have had a sizable community of Mexican immigrants in the parish to which I was assigned. That opportunity required me to learn whatever Spanish I could by a process of immersion and intensive study of the language. Twice I spent time studying in Guadalajara, Mexico.

A side benefit was that I could explore the origins of faith there. That story began in the 1520's with the coming of Hernando Cortez and the Spaniards. I had known nothing of this Mexican history, its Aztec roots and dominance, or of the origin of Catholicism there in that time.

As it turned out, the opportunity gave me the chance to understand a bit of the evangelization that took place there by the Franciscan, the Dominican and the Augustinian missioners that followed in the years after Cortez. While Europe was locked in the struggles of the Protestant Reformation, Spanish missioners were converting a whole indigenous people in another hemisphere.

The Aztec culture that the missioners found revolved around human sacrifice, offered to the benefit of the gods (read "spirits") who controlled and dominated those cultures. Done in the City of Tenochtitlán, located where Mexico City is today, these offerings of human hearts, cut from the victims while still alive, were a frequent and constant core of what was required of oppressed and slave states around the dominant Aztecs.

It was a violent and demonic atmosphere there in that time. The sacrifices were done at the top of pyramid structures, the blood pouring down the steps, the still beating hearts held up for all to see.

Subjugated tribes and conquered soldiers were the primary victims.

When the missioners came, one of the reasons that converts came so easily was that the missioners were able to address directly this violence, by simply saying that the people were now safe from the gods, the spirits.

The missioners taught that, once and for all, that in the cross, the blood of Christ was enough to bring them salvation and would protect them. They quickly perceived that the Body and Blood of Christ would be shared with them in the Eucharist. That sacrifice needed not to be repeated, because the one sacrifice of Christ upon the cross was enough to reach through the centuries to them. That sacrifice on the cross was done once and for all, and it is that moment we now celebrate in every Eucharist.

There was simply no point to what the Aztecs had been doing before.

Again, as with the Korean culture, the liberation of the indigenous peoples of Mexico was clearly bound up with the discovery and ownership of the presence of Jesus Christ in their lives. Never again were they forced to go back to that kind of slavery and oppression, now that they had found true faith in Christ. Never again would they be subject to such a spiritual underworld. This new freedom in Christ was supported in the main by the presence of Our Lady of Guadalupe, in the apparitions that occurred to Saint Juan Diego.

The Power of the Presence of Christ

In the example of these two cultures, we can see clearly that the existence of a God was never the issue in question. In fact, the existence of a spiritual dimension in those cultures spurred the innocent and ordinary citizens of those times to find a way, a connection to God. They could not, until the truth of faith and the Gospel was brought to them. Once brought there, the change in people's lives was often almost instantaneous.

To put it in other terms, throughout the world the discovery of the presence of Christ was an incredible moment of grace, reaching from heaven above. Culture after culture saw this grace touch any who had an openness of heart and a deep seated goodness within their souls.

Throughout history, in culture after culture, these stories have been repeated, often with much martyrdom. However, always the result was that the poor and the humble found the grace to perceive the presence of Christ. Beyond that first moment, this grace was a redeeming and enriching context for a new form of life in the way of the Gospel.

In addition, the spirits, the minions of Satan's kingdom, were defeated by the cross of Jesus Christ. There was a kind of spiritual liberation in culture after culture, that those who found Jesus Christ could possess and thrive within. There are countless more examples from other cultures, spread out over two thousand years.

In a heartbeat, the presence of God's love, this redeeming grace revealed Christ, lifting souls from that sense of spiritual slavery. How easily does the Gospel touch peoples lives in that context. How crystal clear the Good News of Jesus Christ is in such cultural times. How stunning and unexpected is the arrival of grace from above.

3. Orphans

- The message of the cross is foolishness to
those who are perishing, but to us who are
being saved it is the power of God. For it
is written: "I will destroy the wisdom of
the wise, and the learning of the learned I
will set aside." Where is the wise one?
Where is the scribe? Where is the debater
of this age? Has not God made the wisdom
of the world foolish?
1 Corinthians 1:18–20

The Contemporary Dilemma

A dilemma exists here in the 21st Century. As this
culture is evolving in this era, there is often nothing that is seen or felt as the divine. This is what
makes the 21st Century different. There is nothing transcendent, nothing from above. Here is a
climate of secularism, an agnostic milieu. The
grace that would reveal the presence of Christ
somehow remains buried under layer after layer
of agnosticism.

To say that God is dead widely underestimates the
felt absence of anything or anyone spiritual. It is
presumed that there is no creator, no redeemer, no
grace, no forgiveness. In addition, many have ac-

tually given up looking for anything at that spiritual level. Others have bought into a kind of empty existence, assuming that the materialism of the present moment can yield a satisfactory existence. They think: "This is all there is, there isn't anything else." It's a kind of doubled up absence, without either a goal or a passageway to the goal.

As a result, God the Father, and his son Jesus Christ are undiscoverable by many today. There is no evidence, so it seems, of the closeness of God in the TV shows that people see. There is no evidence of the presence of Jesus Christ in the media. There is no evidence that the Holy Spirit might hover anywhere over the struggles today that many are experiencing. Who would even think of going to a church, or talking to a christian about what is lacking in their lives? The grace of all this is buried deeper and deeper.

Not that the evidence doesn't exist anymore. Instead, the secularism is so pervasive that anything spiritual has been long suppressed or forgotten. The secular era has amnesia to the max about Jesus Christ, or the Holy Spirit. There is not even a whiff of God as our Father.

If you cannot yearn for, if you cannot hunger for the presence of God in your life, how will you ever be converted or be completed?

The Satanic, Visible

There is, of course, the Satanic portion of what people experience in this 21st Century. Sometimes it is called science fiction, but always about a demonic presence: aliens, zombies, or extra-terrestrials. Somehow all this weirdness is supposedly acceptable and believable to the culture of the 21st Century. How bizarre that is, given that nothing of divinity can be allowed, only the demonic!

None of this secularism leads upward towards the divine, only downward to what is fragmented and isolating in this postmodern world. None of these demonic and supernatural images leads anywhere towards what will bring a person to conversion in Jesus Christ.

Materialistic life is going nowhere, giving nothing, and yielding no sense of identity. Yet, all the doors and windows that previous cultures had to the divine and the transcendent presumably have now slammed shut for many of the 21st Century, seemingly leaving no clue, or no option. Instead, there is an unbroken invisibility coupled to an unassailable darkness, never before fully felt in this world.

This demonic awareness, portrayed always as if it were fiction or imagination, doesn't lead upward to a theology or to a sense of transcendence, but pretends to be a simple fiction. All the while this portrayal sows the discord, oppression, and chaos of the inverted, alternative universe of Satan.

This is how our generation is different from all those that have gone before us. This era begins with a nothingness; it is content free. There is nothing to which to respond, leaving only an impossibility that could never supposedly draw a person to conversion.

21st Century Orphans

The victims of this era are beyond count. I find most to be less perpetrators than victims. Many are, as it were, embargoed, orphaned by a cultural contagion that doubles the pain and confusion of human existence. This secularism of our times is thus peopled in large part by a kind of orphans, without theology, transcendence or hope.

When I had returned from my five years in Korea, I quickly re-acclimatized to my former environment of Southeastern Minnesota. I remember that one late, fall day towards the end of October, I was driving back to the parish on county roads. As I drove along, I noticed the pumpkins and scarecrows set up in from of the houses along the road, ready for Halloween.

All of a sudden, I caught that they were identical in design to what I had seen in my five years in Asia. Those were just like the totems, symbolic figures to ward off evil spirits. They were exactly

what I had seen in my years in Asia. Having returned back here, in the days just before Halloween, I saw skeletons and black crepe paper
adorning a hidden, universe as if from below.
Only now, they were here with a long forgotten
origin!

Then, I remembered, of course, that our culture
had come from centuries of that kind of practices
in ancient Europe. Our ancestors had dealt with
the same kind of shamanistic awarenesses for
thousands of years. But these ancestor knew both
the existence of a God that they couldn't reach on
their own.

Once Christ was found, that spiritual imprison-
ment was abrogated. Here in this culture, we no
longer know what those totems and symbols rep-
resented, why anyone celebrated their presence at
Halloween, or from what reality they had come.
The roots were still there. However, their signifi-
cance was long gone, having yielded completely to
an environment that knew neither spirits nor divinity. Now all seemed just awash in the hollowness of secularism. While anything of the presence
of Christ with us, any knowledge of Our Father in
heaven was now unacceptable, all those remnants
of superstition were still allowed. Such is a
strangeness today between what is acceptable and
what is not.

This is now a world and a time that defines itself
without a sense of the grace from above that could
redefine us. This is now a world and a time that

can't allow itself to find Christ. This is now a world and a time entering the final stage of re-defining humanity itself as a kind of self centered-ness, a final stage of isolation and being orphaned.

However, we should note that Satan's world is a desperation of delay, filled with many innocents, who will witness to the evil around them, and will begin to turn, heart and soul, seeking the presence of the risen Christ. The end of these times can only be replaced with a new awareness of the very grace that was forgotten and abandoned.

The Context of Grace

The evil of this time, however, will become the bedrock of future evangelization. Grace will not be denied. Grace is more powerful than anything in the 21st Century. Grace, as the love of God for all who would seek to find Him, is ever present, and only grows stronger in denial. The more this world flees, the more the grace from above will be visible in the darkness. The more people are or-phaned within secularism, the more the redeemer will be made visible in the gift of grace.

I believe there will be a stream of conversions, leading many to find hope and purpose, identity and meaning in the only place possible: in the arms of Jesus Christ, in the hands of God the Fa-ther. Even these times hold a bright promise of hope, coming from above, a light in the darkness, a warmth in this cold. This transformation is all beyond anything that anyone think possible now, in this inverted, alternative universe of the 21st Century.

In the end we cannot discount the Holy Spirit at work in our midst these days. In fact, the more discordant the culture becomes, the more Christ and the Spirit will shine in the darkness. The more isolated and humiliated humanity will become in the 21st Century context, the more the search will progress for anyone who seeks to find the presence of the risen Lord, the hidden Christ. The Spirit will provide.

Even the absence of the divine, the invisibility of the transcendent will broadcast the coming of Christ in our midst. Strange as it seems, even the secularism in our midst will have to proclaim that there is a Christ, and will unwillingly telegraph the way to find Him. Grace is the gateway that shines brightly in the midst of denial, the light of Christ in the darkness. The darkness itself will assist in the proclamation of the Gospel.

4. Hiddenness

- Christ Jesus is the image of the invisible God, the firstborn of all creation. For in him were created all things in heaven and on earth, the visible and the invisible, whether thrones or dominions or principalities or powers; all things were created through him and for him. He is before all things, and in him all things hold together. He is the head of the body, the church. He is the beginning, the firstborn from the dead, that in all things he himself might be preeminent. For in him all the fullness was pleased to dwell, and through him to reconcile all things for him, making peace by the blood of his cross through him, whether those on earth or those in heaven. Colossians :15-20

The Presence of Christ

The hidden presence of Christ in our midst is at the very core of who we are as Catholic. Nothing could be more basic than this awareness of Christ with us, that we, as Eucharistic people, sense again and again that the risen Christ walks with us. In every Mass we hear his words spoken not just 2000 years ago, but that are spoken to us now, as the only words that truly make sense in this world.

In each time of prayer, we open our hearts to what Christ tells us, about how we are to thrive in such a realm of confusion about exactly who it is that we are. Each time we receive Communion, we open our hearts and our very lives to this presence of Christ. We walk out the doors at the end of the Mass with a strengthened and renewed sense of Christ's power in our lives.

In every Mass there is an action completed that is exactly needed for our times. Often, we misunderstand, thinking that it is the consecration, the moment of Christ becoming present under the form of bread and wine. We think that is the totality of the action.

The consecration of the bread into the Body of Christ and the wine into the blood of Christ is only the beginning of the action. This action began at the Last Supper climaxed at the crucifixion and the resurrection. The action was and is all one. So today we experience this action that is all one within the corpus of the Mass.

There is the consecration that brings Christ present to us in a most sacred way. Then there is the climax, where in the offering of the great amen, we experience the conclusive moment of Jesus is giving himself to the Father, and that the Father is receiving. Then there is the moment of

Communion when what transpired between the Son and His Father is shared within each of us.

The Mass has the ability to catapult us directly into those moments of the dying and rising of Christ. How different this is from the emptiness of the secular!

Presence in the Midst of Absence

One of the puzzling anomalies of this secular 21st Century is the seeming absence of Christ in our era, even in the face of what we as Catholics sense day in and day out about the very presence of Jesus Christ. On the one hand, that apparent absence of Christ in this culture of today is simply the result of a world that now is so opposed to Jesus Christ that they do not dare to recognize him.

On the other hand, if Christ were admitted and recognized, it would clearly shift priorities in peoples lives. Morality and justice would suddenly reappear. Marriage and family would once again become a priority. The poor would rank first.

This age of secularism has wandered so far from the presence of Christ, that Christ now appears completely if mysteriously forgotten. This generation has even forgotten that they have forgotten, enmeshed in empty wanderings, like someone who neither remembers from where they have come, or where it is that they are now going. For many in these times, the experience of living comes close to being persons, lost in a forest, recognizing nothing, ultimately alone. In these times, there is often no East or West, no North or South, no past or future to hold, no philosophy that works, no truth that lasts. Without an awareness of Jesus Christ, there is no compass or gyroscope, leaving this era a sad, sad realm.

The Protection of the Spirit

However, there is another dimension to this seeming absence of Christ today. This dimension is that we who are disciples of Jesus Christ are in effect hidden away from this world in many ways. Along with having forgotten Christ Himself, the world of the secular appears to forget that Jesus Christ has many disciples in this contemporary world. In fact. we exist below the radar of the postmodern world. We seem too insignificant to be counted.

While the world uses every tactic to humiliate and shame the disciples of Christ, most of us live invisibly, simply following Jesus Christ as best we can. In that, just like Christ, we are somewhat invisible to this world of the secular. We are thought to be irrelevant to what is happening today. We are believed to be completely out of touch with all that is important today. We are thought to be belonging to a completely discredited and outdated superstition. It is assumed that anyone in step with today's world could not possibly believe that there was any substance there to be believed. Could there possibly be any wider abyss between the secular and the Catholics of today?

Hidden, not Absence

This is an astounding situation. Today, we are being subtly persecuted because of our lack of participation in this culture that has lost its way. We have little power today, and certainly none of the financial resources that are the engine of progress. We are gradually being excluded from public education, from corporate and governmental roles, because we are labeled as bigots, somehow opposing the requirements of the LBGTQ doctrine.

I wonder, is this trait of the invisibility of Christ in today's world, not an absence, just a hiddenness? Is this almost a form of protection on God's part, to allow us to live simply, steeped in the pattern of Christ himself?

In truth, we have been invited by the Lord himself to live with our hearts and minds focused on exactly who we are, and why we are here. The call of Christ today is to recognize what our true identity and destiny actually is.

Not that we will not experience the humiliation and shaming that the secular world would impose upon us. Rather I think that we end up strengthening our minds and hearts. We end up possessing a solid sense of community that can come only from the awareness of the hidden presence of the risen Christ in our midst.

The key point is that there is a certain amount of invisibility that Christ gives to his people, protecting them while they deepen themselves in the gifts of the Spirit. This likewise is a part of the grace of God, the love of God that shelters us in these days.

It may seem that we are now invisible and irrelevant to this postmodern world. Instead, what it really means is that we can continue to exist in the realm of grace, protected by the love of God. In this context, we are able to deepen and grow as families and marriages despite existing in the midst of chaos. Even when the doors of this postmodern world remain closed, there remains the open door from above, linking us to the oneness of Christ, with Him who rules our hearts.

To put it another way, for us who are Catholic today, this is not the time of the harvest. Instead it will look like the earth at the time of planting, with no results, seeming to be barren earth. However, in the hiddenness of these times, the growth is within the hearts and souls of the faithful, within our homes and families, Eucharistic to the core!

Sensing the Difference

The key, in this sense of hidden life in Christ, is that we identify concretely the qualities of this postmodern world in which we are living. At at the same time, we are to recognize the very presence of Christ walking with us. There is no possibility of our faith growing and deepening apart from a profound sense of the difference between our faith and this secular era.

There is no room here to neglect the insidious nature of the secular era, about how these times are designed to undermine everything about the grace of God. Having so understood the world in which we are living, we then need to recognize clearly the profound love of God for us that works through the presence of Christ with us.

There is nothing to hold on to in this secular era itself. No truth, no value, no virtue can be maintained today without the presence of Christ alive in our hearts. The understanding of the presence of Christ with us is the lens that will illustrate what the secular era is.

As always, grace, the gateway, is an opening that seems closed to every human potential in these contemporary times. However, because it is from above, grace joins us to the realm of what is beyond the limits of our nature. As a result we know that we belong instead to the realm of of the kingdom of God, a grace that yields, thirty, sixty, or a hundredfold potential, far and above anything within this world. In the Eucharistic presence of Jesus Christ, grace is always at work within us.

5. Camouflaged

- This is how it is with the kingdom of God;
  it is as if a man were to scatter seed on the
  land and would sleep and rise night and
  day and the seed would sprout and grow,
  he knows not how. Of its own accord the
  land yields fruit, first the blade, then the
  ear, then the full grain in the ear. And
  when the grain is ripe, he wields the sickle
  at once, for the harvest has come.
  To what shall we compare the kingdom of
  God, or what parable can we use for it? It
  is like a mustard seed that, when it is sown
  in the ground, is the smallest of all the
  seeds on the earth. But once it is sown, it
  springs up and becomes the largest of
  plants and puts forth large branches, so
  that the birds of the sky can dwell in its
  shade."
  Mark 4:26-32

Grace Seemingly Hidden

If we go looking for the presence of grace in our
world, the grace we seek to find comes close to a
kind of phantasm. Seldom do we get an image
that can help define the parameters of it. Grace, in
this world, is a kind of whisper in amongst an in-

nuendo of noise. Perhaps this is intentional on the part of the Lord above, that grace might best be found somewhere between the dissonance and melodies, in between the images and accents that make up everyday life. In the spaces that this world neglects, there is grace, for all to see.

On the other hand, I know that it is in the miniature that we can best see the beginnings of the immensity of grace. The Gospel spills over in little images and analogies that clearly point to the presence of grace, hidden in this world, hidden but visible only to the eyes of faith. Grace is often revealed in things that are too little to be noticed, and then grow geometrically and serendipitously. The words of the Gospel frame this aspect of grace, again and again.

The Gospel and Grace

Matthew's version of the Gospel overflows with such imagery. In the Sermon on the Mount (5:13-15), Jesus Himself points to several images that clearly reflect the working of grace in our times.

- "You are the salt of the earth. But if salt loses its taste, with what can it be seasoned? It is no longer good for anything but to be thrown out and trampled underfoot. You are the light of the world. A city set on a mountain cannot be hidden. Nor

do they light a lamp and then put it under
a bushel basket; it is set on a lamp stand,
where it gives light to all in the house."

At another point Matthew, Chapter 13.33, speaks
of another pointer to the realm of grace:

- Jesus spoke to them another parable. "The
  kingdom of heaven is like yeast that a
  woman took and mixed with three mea-
  sures of wheat flour until the whole batch
  was leavened."

How ordinary each of these images is: the salt, the
lamp stand, and the yeast. Yet in each of them,
their reach is far beyond what one might expect: a
touch of salt, a lamp in a dark room, or a bit of
yeast. Yet each of these images touches the very
essence of what the grace of God does in our lives,
lifting us up beyond what seems to be the limits of
nature. How could something so small as salt or
yeast have so much effect. The grace of God is the
same. Grace touches and reshapes us in dramatic
ways, beyond what we ourselves seem capable of
doing.

Always there is this element of surprise in the
grace that touches us. Always we are stunned by
what happens when Christ inhabits our lives and
our souls. It is clearly like a single light in a room
full of darkness that draws us into itself. That
light of grace dominates everything of value in the

midst of that darkness. Clearly, what is in miniature in the hands of the Lord can easily become something of immensity in our lives. That is precisely the dimension of grace in our world, even and especially in our times.

A Vision Coupled to a Tornado

Let me cite an example for you, drawn from my local area. There was a small town in the 1880's, struck by a tornado, called Rochester, Minnesota. This storm, as you might imagine, resulted in high casualties. There was no hospital there to turn to in the victims needs.

There was a doctor, however, in this community. His name was Dr. William Worrall Mayo. There was also a religious congregation of Franciscan Sisters in the same community. The head of that community was Mother Mary Alfred Moes.

While the elder Dr. Mayo did not think it possible, Mother Mary Alfred suggested that they should build a hospital. She had apparently come upon this idea in a kind of vision. Dr. Mayo thought that it could never be financed. Sr. Mary Alfred said she would raise the money. She did. The hospital was built, and Dr. William Worrall Mayo and his two sons, Drs. William and Charles, then staffed the hospital, using the Franciscan sisters to help with the nursing.

This is a classic case of something beginning from the smallest of seeds, impossibly small, but destined to become a number one hospital in the country if not in the world, the largest employer in the State of Minnesota, and a city of incredible, improbable growth, all because a single Franciscan sister in the 1880's believed it could be done, and a family of doctors then kept their promise to staff the hospital that was built. What was done, on a kind of wing and a prayer, morphed into something way beyond what could have been imagined in the beginning, with astounding growth, and a national model of exactly what medicine should become in terms of science, research, and responsible health care. All this, from a minuscule idea that a single Franciscan Sister proposed in the 1880's, all this from a result of a tornado.

Salt, Light and Yeast

In essence, this example is a symbol of how grace itself works in our lives. The Holy Spirit touches us, in what often seems a very small way. Then, when we respond with a yes to what it is that we are being called, the grace of the Holy Spirit takes over, and draws us further and further into something of greater proportions. Grace is the energy that the kingdom of God uses to mushroom in our times. Grace is the power of God's love to multiply the yield in the kingdom to thirty, or sixty or a hundredfold, with totally unexpected results.

This example highlights the images from the Scriptures: the salt, the light on a lamp stand, the yeast we add to flour, the mustard seed that looks nothing like the bush to which birds can come to and dwell. This surprise of grace is like the cripple at the pool of Bethesda, the leper isolated from his family, the blind man shouting out to Jesus after many years of blindness. This is the acorn that Paul writes about that will end up an astounding oak tree.

Thus, it happens that a young couple makes a marriage vow together before Christ, without anything more than a rough dream of what that marriage might become. Fifty years later, they sit at their anniversary celebration, looking around at their family, now with a couple dozen grandchildren and great grandchildren. They sit there wondering how all this happened, when all they were doing was living a day at a time, month after month, and year after year. Where did all these blessings come from? This illustration gives a pretty good picture of how grace works in our lives.

The Holy Spirit takes some small, minuscule "yes" on our part, and then helps it burgeon into something far beyond. This is grace at it best, often rising from our failures and struggles, to grow and grow in our lives, surprising us when it happens. We end up unsure of where and why that growth happened. Time and again, we are stunned by what blessings happen within our lives, goodness that we never expected, all out of proportion. Thus, we shake our heads about the subtle intrusion of God's hand in our lives and hearts. Grace has the power to end up beyond all expectations.

The Engine of the Kingdom

This is the kingdom of God in our world. While the world itself flails about in uncertainty and false hope, there, behind it all, the Holy Spirit pours out the grace of the Trinity into lives. The engine of the kingdom of God is divine grace, come from above. God's grace empowers goodness and truth in our world, showing us how sacrifice and dedication blossom forth into miracles and wonders in our midst.

It is of critical importance that the Catholics of the 21st Century awaken to the hidden character of grace that is in our midst, that will break forth in multidimensional ways to lead humanity to the redemption that it now refuses. Because grace lies hidden in our times, we need the eyes of faith to recognize how that grace is present and working both within our parishes and ministries, as well as in the fragmented and fragile dimensions of the secular in the 21st Century.

Grace is both hidden and unexpected today, often only emerging in the midst of failure and defeat.

At the core of things, in the cross of Jesus Christ we hold the secret to the final coming of Christ and the final manifestation of the kingdom of God.

This secular era appears to the Catholic of today to be an almost unstoppable, an inevitable rock-slide into nothingness and hopelessness. Yet it is precisely that context, that we, as Catholic, are to view all that is happening with eyes of faith. In that confusion and uncertainty we to realize that the Holy Spirit will shower us with a constant mist of grace, touching every aspect of our humanity. In these times the Holy Spirit will provoke that improbable, unlikely, and even impossible moment when the kingdom of God will mushroom forth in an exponential revelation of the love that the Father and His only begotten Son have for all of creation.

We are to stand firm in the knowledge of God's love for us, the coming of grace into our midst, and in the certainty and blessing of the final coming of the Kingdom of God. All of this, is the working of grace, the mark of the love of God for creation.

6. The Gateway

- As it was in the days of Noah, so it will be
   in the days of the Son of Man; they were
   eating and drinking, marrying and giving
   in marriage up to the day that Noah en-
   tered the ark, and the flood came and destroyed them all. Similarly, as it was in the
   days of Lot: they were eating, drinking,
   buying, selling, planting, building; on the
   day when Lot left Sodom, fire and brim-
   stone rained from the sky to destroy them
   all. So it will be on the day the Son of Man
   is revealed.
   Luke 17.26-28

Subiaco

The one time I was able to go to Italy, one of my
most memorable moments was a visit to Subiaco,
the founding place where Saint Benedict had be-
gun his religious life. In fact, it was a cave high up
the mountain, a place from where he could watch
over the main roadway far down the valley, leading to Rome.

His cave was not much, seemingly only enough
space in which to sleep, away from the elements.
However, its vantage point was perfect, looking

far down a widening valley that ended in the main road of travel. This was a perfect place to witness the traffic that was coming South into the Roman empire's central peninsula. The vista that Benedict had from that point was vastly expansive, both geographically, and spiritually.

This era of Benedict was a time of the Goths, one of the invaders of the dark ages, who marched down the Italian peninsula into Rome. In addition, it was the breakup of many of the remnants of the Roman Empire that had existed for centuries.

The location of Benedict's cave, the place of the beginnings of the Benedictine way, was a perfect vantage point for what was coming, with a great view. That cave was also a vantage point of what it was that was dying in those times, the long awaited death of the empire that had stood for ages.

The location was also such that it was of critical importance to anyone seeking to fortify their faith in Christ the Lord. From that high vantage point, a sincere disciple of Christ was able to discern exactly what it was that was coming. Subiaco was a place to envision exactly what the future was going to hold for anyone faithful to Christ and the church.

The Vantage Point We Have

This image of Benedict's first cave gives us a similar vantage point for the present times, knowing that the era of the secular, the postmodern times in which we live, would encroach upon the very substance of our Catholicism, imparting its own version of the invasion of the Goths upon us.

We are, strangely enough, as Catholics, the key challenge to these times. Our faith stands as a confrontation to the very self indulgence and self deification that is so present in this 21st Century. This era tries very hard to force our participation in issues such as same sex marriage, artificial birth control, or the breakup of the connection to our sexuality and gender identity. We, as Catholic, stand as the one stubborn obstacle, the one immovable object that remains to the secular world's destruction of all that flows from God's creation.

We as Catholic, by our very theology, stand virtually alone about same sex marriage. We alone uphold the unbreakable goal of openness to children, and the right of parents to direct the education and formation of their children. We alone, in this secular age, have the power in Christ to resist any and all of the efforts to compromise our ways into something that looks a great deal like an image of the antichrist.

If we are true to our faith as Catholic, we will never yield to this destructive and fragmenting climate of the secular. In addition, nor will this climate of the 21st Century bend us to be participants in its ongoing self destruction. We will be the last immovable object of the 21st Century.

The power behind us is not our own strength. Of that power, we have little. If there is any power in this world, it is not the supposedly unstoppable force of the secular.

Rather, the power over all is the presence of Christ with us, and the gift of grace raining down over us. We as Catholic can have a clear grasp of what that truth means for us, and how that truth defines who and what we are. In truth, we hold our stance with a singularity and a solidarity that is of the essence of our faith today.

If we live within the grace of Jesus Christ, if we put ourselves into the way of Christ, we remain one force that Satan's inverted alternative universe cannot destroy. This is the story of the power of grace, that it cannot be overwhelmed by anything in this world. This grace comes from above, from the cross of Christ itself, from the presence of Jesus Christ in our midst, from our Father in heaven, and from His love for us.

The Provocation in the Cross

This victory in Christ is so much so that, if we live out our Catholic faith to the max, we will provoke the very coming of the Lord in the final days. Our fidelity will expose with clarity the hidden refusal to acknowledge that Jesus Christ is Lord of heaven and earth.

We need to think this through a little. I am saying that the only real obstacle to the final coming of Christ, and to the final proclamation of the kingdom of God is our own weakness and lack of faith in the presence of Christ with us. That presence alone will allow the gift of grace to work within us.

Satan has neither a grasp of how to attain victory nor any plan other than to stall Christ's final coming. All he can do is to try to subvert the truth of the cross of victory into a kind of delaying action.

In fact, the chaos and evil of these times wilts in the face of the grace that the Father has placed deep within us. The cross of Christ has made available unassailable gifts to us to deal with these times. If we would turn towards what is granted to us with all our hearts, Christ will immediately and powerfully come and reign with us for all the world to see. This is true, despite all the suffering and self sacrifice that may be required of us, while this world augers its way to self destruction.

The Gateway is Open

Let me be clear. The issue is not that these times are something of which to be frightened. After all, we are disciples of Jesus Christ, who has already won the victory over death and sin. The cross is the definitive moment where the victory is anchored forever.

We are children of the Father, and have been reborn into the new creation that is yet to be completely unveiled. In addition, the Holy Spirit hovers over us, enlightening our journey. In no way, are we the doormats of secularism. We need to own the inheritance that is indeed ours. All this exists in the face of what often camouflages itself as our certain defeat from the hands of a supposedly invincible secularism!

The agnosticism of our times is a journey of self destruction.

This secular era is the total denial of the Lordship of Jesus Christ and that of the Father. Despite its self portrayal as a kind of grand technological and scientific advancement of humanity, the secularism of the 21st Century looks a great deal more like a flea bitten, pockmarked and rust infected zone of deception, untruth, and self contradiction. That secularism is going nowhere other than into a previously and completely unaddressed zone of nothingness. Truly, secularism is the host to the absurd, inverted alternative universe of Satan. That universe ends in abortion, sterility, violence, addiction and suicide.

21st Century Catholic

We, as Catholic, need two skills for these times. First, we need to recognize the secular era for exactly what it is. There can be no sugar coated compromise with that secularism. Nor can there be any kind of delusional hope that thinks only in horizontal human terms. Secondly, we, as catholics, need to be keenly aware of the gifts and tools handed us by Christ and the Holy Spirit so that we can adequately recognize these times, and constantly rise above the emptiness and dissolution that is emerging in this century.

Both of these skills will give the endurance to witness the futile struggles of this secular world as it chaotically collapses into its final decline, whiplashing itself in violence and agony to all around it. In the midst of such dissolution, what Christ has set aside for us puts us on an incredible journey, one filled with truth and meaning, one driven by the power of God's grace. Living solely for Christ preserves all that is good within us, and fills us with a destiny and an identity beyond anything that is merely human.

Our Brothers and Sisters, Often Victims

Indeed, this secular age is an easily irresistible target of mockery, were it not for the fact of the countless victims, who understand little of the evil in which they are being trapped. Our presence has to be the witness to the only passageway through that self destruction.

Our task is to help these times look beyond the horizontal, to look upward to the grace and truth flowing downward from above. Thus results our need to identify clearly what this secularism is, and what there is to turn to, in response.

In summary, to be Catholic in this 21st Century can yield us all that we need to be able to deal with, to endure, and to overcome whatever frag-mentation the secularism of this era would seek to inflict upon us. On top of that, we stand to be a one voice to which the countless victims of this era will be able to turn. Indeed, we are at our own Subiaco.

Transcendence and Grace

What is required of us is a knowledge of what it is that comes from above, We need a sense of what it is that God has hidden deep within us. What comes from above is the only gift that can remake us into the new creation that Saint Paul talks about.

In each of us, as disciples, there is this transcen-dental dimension rooted within us of which the world knows nothing. Our conversion and our

Sacraments of Initiation awaken this dimension deep within our souls.

That gift is the gift of grace, the palpable love of God that allows us to begin to live at the level that Our Father in heaven has intended for us from before the beginning of all creation. This hidden, essential piece to our existence is what grace is all about. This grace, this love of God, manifests itself in the Father's sending of his Son to us. Grace unveils itself in Christ's dying on the cross for us, and hovers over us as the Holy Spirit in our lives. Despite whatever trauma we face, whatever trials we might be enduring, this love from above only deepens more and more in our hearts.

This grace is something without which we would have no hope of ever reaching the heart of goodness and truth that we know should be deeply rooted within us. Grace is God's never ending love for us, packaged up and planted deep within us. We can have some sense of its existence within us, but this grace remains dormant in our lives, awaiting the intrinsic changes within us that liberate it. This grace dissolves humanity's never ending shame. Grace is the gateway that Christ's sacrifice on the cross opened.

Grace changes us to make us become something beyond what our human nature allows. Our nature never quite gets us there. Humanity by itself is stuck in a loop of endless effort to become what we can see in our natures, but cannot get our arms around to possess.

Grace then is the gateway, particularly in this era of the secular, that opens the pathway for us to become exactly what it is that Our Father in heaven had in mind for us from the beginning. Grace is the love of the Son in his total gift on the cross to the Father, and the love of the Father so complete that this love raised up his Son from the dead. In that love, the Holy Spirit engulfs and saturates the humanity and the nature of all who say yes to this oneness with the Trinity.

This is the stunning development, the surprising transformation of those who access the gift of grace. This gift is precisely what lifts us above and beyond the dismal and frantic secularism of the 21st Century, and points us into the new kingdom, the kingdom of God. This gift of grace is what, by itself, overcomes and outdoes all of the evil and vacillations of this era. One by one, we must evaluate the weight of grace over against the emptiness of the era of the secular, and learn to see with the eyes of faith, as Jesus taught!

- Jesus taught them a lesson. "Consider the fig tree and all the other trees. When their buds burst open, you see for yourselves and know that summer is now near; in the same way, when you see these things happening, know that the kingdom of God is near."
  Luke 21:29-31

7. Extravagance

- For if by that one person's transgression the many died, how much more did the grace of God and the gracious gift of the one person Jesus Christ overflow for the many. And the gift is not like the result of the one person's sinning. For after one sin there was the judgment that brought condemnation; but the gift, after many transgressions, brought acquittal. For if, by the transgression of one person, death came to reign through that one, how much more will those who receive the abundance of grace and of the gift of justification come to reign in life through the one person Jesus Christ.
Romans 5:15-17

Our Experience of Grace

In order to think about the grace in our lives, let's start from our experience. The fact is, we are not strangers to the reality of grace, but more often than not, we don't perceive this hidden realm of divine grace within which we live. The love of God is often content to live within us somehow unnoticed and unrecognized for a time. Then this grace surprises us at how much it had been active and instrumentals all along.

Sometimes, only in retrospect do we sense the subtle, but often, dramatic difference that God's grace makes in our lives. There is often a childlike character of the disciples of Christ that exists within this gift of grace. We are sometimes without an awareness or clear ownership of all that has come to us from above.

I sometimes suspect that only with our death will we fully recognize the presence of Christ, and the gift of grace that he has brought to us in our time in this world. Only then will we fully recognize the radiance of the love of the Holy Spirit that was at work throughout the days of our worldly lives. Probably at that time, we will awaken to the full extent to which Our Father in heaven has gone to protect us, his children in faith. I suspect that at that time we will obtain a full awareness of the extent of Christ's sacrifice for us. Only then will we awaken completely to how the fire of the Holy Spirit had burned continuously in all our weakness and failure. We are often just children traipsing unaware through the daisies and carnations of divine grace that have surrounded us in this existence.

The Silver Ribbon of Grace

God's grace within us awakens with a kind of humble "yes" to God, sometimes without much of any knowledge of where that yes will lead, or to what we will become as a result. That yes we make is often nothing more than the nose of the camel under the tent. We say yes in a kind of trust, not knowing how our life will unfold from that, what traps and struggles we will end up avoiding, or what blessings will descend upon us. This yes that we make is a kind of silver ribbon, weaving in and out of our days, all the way to the end of our lives.

The Scriptures are laced through with examples of this kind of a yes. There was Abraham, saying yes to God's test, inviting him to sacrifice his son, Isaac. In the end of that, in His son, Isaac, Abraham ended up being the father of all the peoples of God. His response was in total faith, in total trust and obedience, without any guarantees. The results were beyond imagining: "More numerous than the stars in the sky." There is an astounding extravagance to grace that's way beyond us.

Then, there was Samuel, just a child, saying to God's call, "Here I am," after several attempts to respond to the high priest whom he had thought was calling him, but wasn't. Again, Samuel knew not where this was to lead, all the way to the coronation of David, as king of Israel, and the forefather of the Messiah, Jesus.

Each of the prophets began by saying yes to God's call. They all struggled with it, Isaiah, for example, saying "Depart from me, I am a sinner." Yet in the end, each of the prophets, by their yes, ended up pointing the way to the one who was to come, Jesus Christ. Beyond that, each of the prophets modeled the cross that was to come as well, by their very own deaths. There is an astounding extravagance to grace that's way beyond us.

Then there was Mary, invited to an incomprehensible and inconceivable challenge, without a clue where it would lead. She probably never did account for all the consequences of her willingness to serve, at least, until the resurrection of her son. Once again there is that extravagance of grace.

Then there were those fishermen, plying their trade at the Sea of Galilee. Jesus said, "Come follow me." Even with the presence of Christ with them, they needed additional instruction and explanation to understand. We might be able to imagine that even the high priests and the pharisees might have understood Christ better than they did. After all, those pharisees and high priests knew exactly what his message entailed, and sought to find a way to stop what the Messiah of Israel was teaching.

None of these who were called knew how or why they were to respond to the call of the Lord. Few of them were plucked from the elite, from the brightest and the best in terms of the world. Each of them was a surprise, both to the world, and to themselves. All of them were touched by something from above, something unexpected in this world. In essence, they were pulled into the love of God for the sake of this world. They were each part of the magnetism of divine grace, eventual witnesses to the extravagance of grace.

In the end, all of them trusted, and went with it on a journey they could never had imagined beforehand. In the end, what they experienced was to be touched by divine grace from above, that would remake who they were and to what they would become. That's the love of God at work in them, the grace of the divine, reshaping and completing their humanity in divine terms.

What I've Learned in My Own Experience

That's the same grace that touches each of us. My own experience in this regard always started with the thought in my mind: "What have I gotten myself into now!"

Around the tenth of June, in 1964, after a difficult first year of theology school, I remember, having been invited to become the chaplain for the summer, at Hok Si La Boy Scout Camp. I remember driving into the camp, myself having barely even been a boy scout. I think I might have gotten one step beyond tenderfoot when I was a kid, with no merit badges. I couldn't even imagine getting an eagle award such as my brother had worked towards. I remember driving into the camp in my 57 Chevy, thinking "What have I gotten myself into now?" And yet, that experience changed the next three years of theology study, as well as those first years of the priesthood. That experience taught me to think of theology in terms of those that I would hopefully someday be serving. That experience got me out of the book world into a practical world of sharing of stories.

Another example: one day in November of 1975, I foolishly volunteered to take over the diocesan newspaper, while I was still in school administration. I knew nothing of publishing, writing headlines, layout, or the design of newspapers. I didn't know what a compugraphic was, or how to paste up a newspaper. At that time, the publication was a weekly. Needless to say. I must have been out of my mind to have said yes to that task.

In the process I introduced a first computerized database mailing list to the distribution, done not without one basic mistake. Do you know how many "John Smiths" there are in a diocese, and that you can't tell one from another without the middle initial? Again, after a steep and painful learning curve, I realized that the Lord had been there to help me all the way into this misadventure. That had to have been the grace of God, reaching out to guide me.

In late October of 1983, I got on a flight from New York City to Seoul, Korea, knowing not one word of the Korean language, with zip experience of serving in the missionary world of Maryknoll. That journey was a 26 hour flight, with half of that time in layovers at airports. Because of crossing the international dateline, I arrived about an hour before I had left, 25 hours after I had departed.

I remember the ride from the airport to the Maryknoll house in Seoul, having arrived in a country still on a war footing with North Korea, watching heavily armed soldiers, leading guard dogs, searching the sides of the roads for spies and invaders. I thought to myself, "What on earth am I doing here?"

Again, my experience there turned out to be an experience in the one country that was growing in a time similar to that of the Acts of the Apostles, a country with hearts and minds open to becoming Catholic. I witnessed hundreds and hundreds of adult baptisms.

On about June 21, 1990, I remember driving down a county road after a short summer thunderstorm, driving down what would become 50th Avenue in Rochester, MN, crossing Kings Run Creek as it was overflowing from the rain, wondering what I had gotten myself into this time, having virtually no parish experience, having been asked to start a new parish in those suburbs. Curiously there was no plan, no records or books on how to start a parish. I was to build a school as well, and I realized that day that I probably was not qualified to be doing such a task. I still don't know how that happened, other than attribute it to the grace of God, as it was way beyond my abilities.

On about Oct. 21, 2003, I left that parish I had built, and moved to Queen of Angels Church in Austin, MN. The parish had a sizable population from Mexico. At 62, I knew it was not likely that I could pick up enough of that language to become fluent. Again, I had gotten myself into something that deep down I knew would be beyond me.

In the end, by the grace of God, I was able to begin a small in-parish community, called the Neo Catecumenal Way. This movement tipped the scales for the Hispanic community, and eventually touched even the Anglo community of the parish to a new and combined sense of ownership within the parish. None of that, on my part, is other than a first yes to what was to come, something far beyond what I was able to do.

The Role of Grace in Our Lives

The only thing that ties the above personal paragraphs together is the role of grace. There I was, an introvert, not great at communication, and was likely to keep problems bottled up within me. Still, I knew I was called to do things I didn't think I could do, constantly thrown into ministries to which I had foolishly said yes.

To this day, I still am keenly aware that most of what I encountered in these 50 plus years of priesthood was beyond what I was capable of doing. If God had asked me in the beginning my best opinion on whether I could accomplish these things, I probably would have told him honestly that I didn't have what would be required to have done any of these things. I probably would have explained that there were many others who had the better personalities, the better organizational skills, and the more outgoing character, and with greater sanctity than me.

I still think that God has a sort of carelessness in his call. It seems He doesn't care whom he calls, but simply knows his grace is sufficient, and that we are covered, as disciples of Christ, for any and all of our failures and insufficiencies. His grace fills in the gaps in each of us. In fact, it is Christ Himself who takes each of us, and lifts us upwards into the identity and character that he wants, in order to bring about His new kingdom.

Grace at Work, Again and Again

This is exactly the character of grace that is at work within all of us. What I experienced is nothing exceptional. I have seen the impact of grace repeatedly in the lives of those with whom I have worked.

In my years as a priest principal in Catholic high schools, I witnessed parents, for the most part untrained and non-experts in the challenges of raising children or teenagers. I deeply respected them in their roles, because over and over they made good choices to have healthy families, often facing difficult dilemmas. I have witnessed the workings of grace within fathers and mothers, doing exactly what their children needed in order to cope with the struggles of family life. I have known parents to be able to say exactly the right thing at the right moment to their son or daughter, just when they needed to hear it.

Where did that all come from, except from divine grace, from above, planted firmly within their role as parents, Christ walking with them. They never gave up on their children!

In addition I have witnessed husbands and wives struggle with the challenges of marriage. I often saw that they never gave up on their spouse, were able to forgive anything, were willing to start over in their relationships, and were able to go through huge tragedies. Yet they would still have a sense of balance and spiritual strength. Where does that come from, except from above, except from the presence of Christ with them, except from the shower of grace from the Holy Spirit at times of need.

I haver watched many who have lost their way spiritually, through sin, addiction, or basic compromises with these times, and then fight their way back into the faith. I have seen people on their deathbed who lived lost lives, who at the last moments discovered Christ's forgiveness. I have seen others struggle with alcohol for years, finally find the grace, the astounding grace to begin recovery.

I have seen others, who thought they were totally lost from God's love, discover that they are now blessed and embraced by God's love. For some, it was an amazing journey that for years had no upward movement, until one day God's love brought them back with such grace that it was almost unbelievable, absolutely miraculous.

The premier instance of God's grace is, of course, how Mary was totally protected from sin by virtue of her role in the divine mystery of the incarnation of her son, yet to be born. While her situation was vastly different in character than ours, that situation was still an infusion of divine love, albeit the highest level of grace ever to have been experienced — given the importance of that moment in salvation history.

The Surprise of Grace

Grace is not rare, it is plentiful. Grace is an extravagance in this world. Grace remains hidden from our world, but is astoundingly visible to anyone who lives with a sense of hope, commitment or dedication to Christ in these times. At times, we who are Catholic, as disciples of Christ in this world are slow to sense that we live in a grace touched environment. We often finally realize that time and again we have been prevented from the harmful or chaotic experience that could have happened, that would have happened were it not for the grace of God. We live in the continuing shower of goodness from the Holy Spirit, often only realizing it in retrospect.

Often times we have a clear sense of our sinfulness, and of the forgiveness that Christ gives to us who are disciples. Sometimes we feel as if we might barely snag the bottom rung of purgatory in the end. That moment of our forgiveness is often the beginning of our experience of God's grace.

Yet, an important part of this grace is our discovery of new life, of the new creation that the dying and rising of Christ has brought to us. We often sense the forgiveness, but not where that grace will lead us. Grace opens up for us the realm from above, the grace touched existence of discipleship. That's almost too good to be believed when we realize what God's love is doing for us.

What's most Difficult to Believe

Once again, we are faced with the most amazing truth, that we are loved by God, in the Father, Son and Spirit. Yet, we find it difficult to let ourselves believe that this love is the most real part of our existence in Christ.

Imagine if you would, the experiences of the first Christians when Paul and the other Apostles preached the new creation, the new life in Christ. My sense is that what Christianity brought to those first Christians was way beyond their everyday experiences of Roman life, either as slaves or as victims of the Roman conquest.

The first Christians found not only forgiveness of sins, for whatever had been the evils and degradation of their lives before. They found that all those things are not only forgiven, but that they themselves were being raised to a level of identity that could have come from nowhere else except from Jesus Christ Himself.

Not only were they freed from their sins of their past, they now found a dignity and worth revealed to them in the cross of Christ. They discovered the Father's love for his children, and the Spirit's revelation of their intrinsic goodness, shown nowhere else but in the Christian community.

It's a two step awakening: first, forgiveness from sin, then secondly, an awareness of God's grace from above, both parts being actually one and the same.

Grace marks a start in a new and different kind of life, new to this world in the coming of Jesus Christ. This life of grace takes human nature, impossible to unify, and reshapes it in the hands of our Savior. This life of grace allows the sincere person of faith to rise to a new level of living, a level now to be lived in the care of Jesus Christ.

This awakening is so beyond our expectations that it seems the most difficult piece of what we are called to believe! Yet, each of us, when we look closely with the eyes of faith, can recognize instantly that the grace of Christ lifts us to a different realm in this world. Eventually we are brought to an acknowledgement that God's love is the most real part of who and what we are.

8. Hollowness

- Behold, I stand at the door and knock. If
  anyone hears my voice and opens the door,
  then I will enter his house and dine with
  him, and he with me."
  Revelation 3:20

A Parable of Grace

There was a story I heard long ago, whose source
I no longer remember.

It seems there was a man who was seeking the
meaning of life. He decided to approach a holy
man, a hermit who lived up the mountain, and so
journeyed there to consult with him.

Upon approaching the holy man with his question, the holy man asked him first to do him a fa-
vor. He asked that he take a bucket down to the
stream below, fill it with water and bring it back
to him.

The man agreed, thinking it to be a very simple
request. However, arriving at the stream, the man
realized that the bucket, very old, had holes in it.
The man filled the bucket with water and climbed

back up the mountain, to no avail, because the water had all leaked out during the climb.

The holy man asked him to try again, which the man did. He went faster this time, but still to no avail. The bucket leaked out all of the water a second time.

This did not stop the holy man from requesting a third attempt, to which the man agreed he would try one last time. This time the man ran as fast as he could with the bucket full of water, splashing water repeatedly over the brim, losing the rest of the water to the leaks. Again he arrived with the bucket empty.

He tossed it down, saying that this bucket was worthless, that it could not be used for this purpose. The holy man then said, "Look at the bucket. It is now perfectly clean. In all of your failure, you have cleansed the bucket."

Our Souls

It's the bucket that caught my attention in the above parable, washed clean, but by itself of no lasting use. In a strange way, that bucket is a symbol of our human soul.

I suspect that our soul has been designed by God specifically to be incomplete, hollow at its core. In our souls, there is a part missing at its very center. The hollowness of our soul, as created by God, was not an accidental omission, not a mistake, not the result of just Adam and Eve's fall. This hollowness at the core of our soul was not some sort of plan B by God, to provide us with a way back, in order to somehow make us turn back to the Lord, when all else failed with Adam and Eve.

On the contrary, our creation had to be this way. After all, we are not God, we are dependent beings by our very nature. We do not exist on our own. Our being is only explicable with our origin from above, derivative from the One who made us.

Think of it in this way: body and soul are like a precision instrument engineered with the key piece missing. This key piece, that is needed, has to be supplied from above. By ourselves, with this intrinsic hollowness deep within our souls, we are as hopeless as an engine without a starter. In truth we have been designed to require the one, key component that fits precisely at the exact center of our souls. However, that key is missing.

The Missing Piece Today

Each person, living in these postmodern times, experiences this hollowness, and strives again and again to find the missing piece. This piece alone can provide the only way that life can take on its full meaning. This is the hidden piece within ourselves that would totally complete us as human beings.

In addition, there is often a kind of desperation to somehow cover that emptiness at the heart of our lives. Nothing we put there on our own really fits. Nothing in our experience is enough to complete ourselves. As good as we find this world, at the end of the day there is always something more. We are almost always in search for something just beyond our grasp that could define us, tell us who and what we are, and most of all, why we are here. Nothing we can do on our own bridges that gap.

Like that bucket hauling the water, we need first of all to cease attempting to satisfy by ourselves this heartfelt need that lies at the root of our being. To overcome that emptiness with the things of this world fails, because nothing on our own really fits the center of our souls.

The First Steps We need to Take

There is a simple little series of steps we need to take in order to deal with this intrinsic sense of hollowness that haunts us deep down. Each step usually comes about because God's love has opened the gateways of grace to us in advance.

The first step is almost always to turn from our sins, to confess our guilt, and to seek the forgiveness from Christ, a kind of first step similar to the cleansing of that bucket! Our sins bring us pain and dissatisfaction. The deeper into our sins we go, the greater that sense of something being terribly wrong with who and what we are. We litter our souls with the debris of our disordered desires and actions, our guilt and our shame. To acknowledge that sinfulness is the initial action of turning to Christ.

Then, in the next step, once we have cleared away the debris and cobwebs in our hearts, we need to make sure that nothing else is at the center of our lives. We have to stop the attempt to fill ourselves with the goods of this world, with the horizontal struggles at activity and experiences that we use to escape from the limits of our power. We have to first cease trying to find things to try to fill up the nothingness, the hollowness that resides within us. Again and again, we find that we have to let go of something that we thought would cover that empty spot at dead center.

This step is terrifying if we are just on our own, absent any sense of God's love and grace. At the end of the day, by ourselves we lack the ability to complete ourselves. We are just created beings, and that emptiness that we can't fill is pretty scary. We are just creatures without a central core!

The Key Step

Then the third step is to invite Jesus Christ to come and be the center of who we are, to take up residence at the very core of our being. The presence of the risen Christ is precisely the piece deep within us that is missing. This is the piece that we have been designed for by God, that we often tried to fill with any other thing that we can find. The presence of Christ dovetails exactly with the hollowness of our souls, filling and completing us to the point of the identity that we have been intended to become from before our creation. Once Christ reigns at the center of our lives, we know who we are and why we are here.

Christ's presence is an exact fit for the center of our souls. We have been engineered, as it were, for this final piece of who and what we are, from the very beginning of our existence.

Only in Christ can we be complete. Only in Christ do we have a source of hope for what we are to become in this world. Only in Christ is our identity finally complete. Only in Christ, can we find the spirit of peace and joy that is so lacking to us in this world. Only in Christ can we truly cease to be afraid for our fragile and temporary existence. Only in Christ, do we ultimately know our exact, final and permanent identity in this world.

Once We Have Found Christ

The fourth step in this journey up the mountain is to allow the grace of the Holy Spirit to guide and direct our daily lives. Actually, that grace will have been instrumental at every step of our existence, even though we probably didn't realize it at first.

Once we have invited Christ into the house of our souls, his grace is the engine of who and what we are to become, how we are to serve, what mission in this life we can do. This grace of God is the power of his love, to lead us step by step into the kingdom of God. This grace from above will teach us how to live in that kingdom here in this world, and to expect the realm of miracle to be a part of our daily lives.

One of the keys of this fourth step is the Mass and the Eucharist. The Mass and Eucharist totally cements this presence of Christ to our souls, and invokes the grace of the Holy Spirit, not in the periphery, but in the essence of our identity. Over the repeated experience of Christ with us in the Mass, and in the reception of the Eucharist, we find ourselves prospering in the ways of faith, now living in this realm of miracle.

A corollary to the experience of the Mass and Eucharist is the Sacrament of Confession, that we let nothing of our former ways, nothing of the failed attempts to fill up the nothingness at our core to

come back into our lives. We are to keep the
house swept clean for Christ to dwell within us.

The Eighth Day of Creation

We have been designed by our creator in such a
way that only one thing will satisfy us, and that is
to be united with Christ Himself. To place Christ
at the center of our lives is the final step in our
creation, that will make us into the creature the
Father intended. When we allow Christ to be at
the center, we are on the eighth day of creation.

In essence, we have been created so that the grace
of our Lord Jesus Christ, can touch and activate
our fragile and fragmented human nature. His
presence will ultimately lead us into the very identity and destiny of children of God. Christ alone
can make us a part of the new way of living, and
bring us to a full participant of the kingdom of
God.

All of this is the result of Our Father in heaven,
loving us so much that he sent his Son for our redemption. All of this is the result of Christ Jesus,
giving Himself so totally, that we can understand
something of how much we have been loved. All
of this is the result of the Holy Spirit, the Love
between Father and Son, saturating us in a constant mist of truth and goodness until we can all
be joined, complete with each other in eternal life.

9. Paradox

- Indeed, the word of God is living and effective, sharper than any two-edged sword, penetrating even between soul and spirit, joints and marrow, and able to discern reflections and thoughts of the heart. No creature is concealed from him, but everything is naked and exposed to the eyes of him to whom we must render an account.
Hebrews 4:12-13

Grace, More than Forgiveness

In trying to understand the grace that has touched us, we need to dig a little deeper. God's grace doesn't stop for us with just the forgiveness of sins. Instead, grace opens a passageway into the kingdom of God. This passageway begins with an awareness of our sinfulness, but then proceeds far beyond that initial awareness.

We easily recognize at first that we have be lifted from the abyss of our sinfulness by God's grace and love. We all become keenly aware of having been rescued from a totally deserved abandonment, with no hope within ourselves of escaping from being totally lost. We end up eternally grateful for what Christ has done for us, lifting us from the abyss of our sins.

The Double Illumination of Grace

However, could grace ever really be more? Is God's grace just there for our forgiveness, or is there something more?

There is something about becoming or being a disciple of Christ. The experience of becoming a disciple contains a kind of ambiguity. This is a paradox that stays with us throughout our faith life, one that we discovered when we first opened our hearts to Christ.

When we finally open ourselves to the love of Christ, we first have the deepest awareness of our fallen state. We are astounded by the truth about ourselves, that despite our best efforts, we found ways to twist or pervert who we were. There arises within us a deep sense of shame, a profound distain for what we have done to ourselves, to those we were to love, and to God's entire creation.

This experience shows up, first of all, in how we hurt one another. Usually the ones we love are the ones that we most hurt. Then, we turn inward to become aware that we have spoiled and stained our own soul by what we have done, especially to those whom we should have loved deeply. The awareness hurts even more because we can't erase the memory, we can't undo what we did. Often we drag around the baggage of our sinfulness day by day. It is often an accumulation that is a huge burden to carry just by ourselves. At first, we do try to do it by ourselves!

Then, one day we have to stop. We don't want to be that person that we have become, and we know that we can't really go on unless we change somehow. We finally reach the point where we know that we need someone from above. This is the humble moment of grace within us.

Finding Our Redeemer

It is usually at that point that we somehow meet the Christ who walks in our midst. We often don't recognize Him. Often, Christ hides Himself within another person near us through whom He speaks. Occasionally his appearance is dramatic. Other times, less so.

It can be a lightning strike or a gentle fog come upon us. Either way, it is the presence of Christ, even if we do not recognize that it is Christ.

It might be through one that we have hurt. It might be through a chance meeting of some stranger whose words are just right. It may have been an angel in disguise. It could have even been a total meltdown in which we give up our pride

and know that everything we thought we were no
longer exists.

To Make Matter Worse

The tragedy of the 21st Century often centers on
the absence, the almost total supression of conscience, without which one can have no concept
of their sinfulness. Without a sense of our sinfulness, we are blind to all that is spiritual. Hence
the portal to the paradox can remain closed. It can
happen that our conscience has been anesthetized
by our egotistical desires, in order to have everything our way in this life. How awful that consequence!

Yet, that portal is not invincible. Most often, that
denial is outwaited by the patience of the Lord,
who simply waits for the struts and supports of
the denial to give way. For most, there is an inevitable moment of our internal collapse where we
can no longer deceive ourselves about our state,
or about who and what we have become.

At that point, we are dead within, and we know it.
We have nowhere else to turn. We can't fix the
past. We can't pretend that what we did was not
our own responsibility. We have no answer to
what has become our state of mind.

Witness St. Paul, blinded by that moment of truth
on the road to Damascus, when all of a sudden he
realized, in a revelation by Christ, that all that he

had done and was doing, was precisely the opposite of what he should have been doing. All at once, he knew that all those he had arrested, all those he had opposed, his every action, plus all the words he had spoken — none of it was right. None of it was good. All of it was sin! No wonder he experienced a kind of temporary blindness! No wonder it was a ten year journey for him to become the missionary that he became.

The 180 Degree Turn

However, there is some point when we become aware that there needs to be something other than what we have been experiencing. This is almost always a dramatic moment for us. We find that there is something that is 180 degrees opposite to how we have been living, and that how we are living now is precisely in the wrong. The experience is scary to us. The question becomes, "What's happening to me?"

Christ may not even reveal Himself, but you know that there is someone, something that just happened, totally out of sync with the failures of my past, something that suggests goodness, that promises a possibility of peace.

But then, it goes even further. Then we become aware that there might just be a possibility that in Christ, our life might be changed. Usually at this point we are stunned, not just the awareness of our sins, but by a sense of goodness, placed near us somehow.

This is the moment of illumination. This is the most stunning moment when we come to understand that Christ is real and present to us, bringing us the paradox of both forgiveness for our sins and the grace to rise above. Here lies the paradox.

Totally undeserved, flat in the face of our sins, there appears a pathway of hope, surprisingly real in our heart. We become aware that this new awareness has come from somewhere we never expected. Thus in the depth of our sins, we find ourselves called to a new beginning, one we didn't earn, one we didn't deserve, one that only could have come to us from above. Then, the broken fragments of our lives and our identity, strangely start to fall into place for us. Lastly, we discover that there is even a new identity in Christ that will reshape and remake us.

There is Even More

From that point forward, we carry this paradox, that despite our sins, we know we are loved in Christ, and we are astounded. We discover what the death of Christ on the Cross has done for us, to both ends of the paradox, that somehow, by his dying, he gave us a way out of the sins of our past, and into a new life with Him.

This new life we begin at that point is the life of grace, and our heart begins to fill with gratitude rather than resentment, with a spirit of joy rather than one of discouragement, with an inner peace rather than with the strife of our past. Now there is a spirit of hope that envelopes us like the sunrise.

Imagine the one crucified by the side of Christ, as they were both hanging on their crosses. That moment with Christ was everything, start to finish, when Jesus said to him that he was to be with him in paradise that very day.

It is truly an astounding discovery that in the cross of Jesus Christ, God our Father has cemented our lives into a new form and shape. Our discovery leads us beyond all the brokenness of our nature, into a new identity. The cross pulls us beyond our nature into something we didn't earn, or into a place that we can't explain how or why it was given to us. This is the part of grace hidden within the forgiveness that Christ has brought to us. Grace alters who we are and how we live, breaking us away from the puny egoism of our inherited natures. This immense gift leads us to begin to live a way now touched by the love of Christ and His Father. This is the breathtaking gift of grace that the Holy Spirit begins to pour out into our souls. This lifts us far beyond the forgiveness we had come to know at the beginning of our conversion.

Experiencing the Paradox Over and Over

In a further part of experiencing this paradox of forgiveness and grace, we discover even more. We come to understand that our Father in heaven sent his son precisely for this reason, to die and to rise so that we might know both parts of our redemption. We are awakened to both our rescue from sin, and our having been lifted up to newness with Christ on the cross.

We are often more articulate about our sinful past than about the miracle of grace that now touches us. It's almost too good to be true, and there are almost no words enough to describe that gift. That is grace! Grace is what we know when we run out of words!

Even more, this moment of paradox is offered to us in the Mass. Through the Eucharist, this central moment is placed before us that we would never forget from where we have come, and to what we have now become. This is the stunning discovery that captures every aspect of our creation. For the rest of our lives, we are left breathless. This is the true moment of the paradox.

In every Eucharist, we recapitulate our journey in this strange paradox that we, who are absolutely undeserving, have somehow been lifted up by the love of Christ and our Father in heaven. How impossible! How totally unexpected! How beyond our comprehension!

Our heritage from the past has always been to emphasize the sinful part that we have been rescued from, and to somewhat neglect the gift of new life of which we have been called to be a part. This emphasis is understandable, given the immensity of our failures, our recidivism and our inability to focus clearly on this new life to which we have been called.

At the same time, we need to own the immensity of change that has happened in our souls, thanks to what Christ has done on the cross, and continues to do for us within the Eucharist. His resurrection is real, his presence is genuinely authentic. That presence deeply insinuates itself into our souls.

In addition, we have the constant memory of those first Christians of the Roman empire that were converted and baptized. These first Christians became absolutely enamored of the rescue that the waters of baptism brought to them and the conversion that was symbolized at the heart of those waters. They were willing to give up their lives for the sake of this new way, this paradox of which they had become a part. Those first disciples found something in addition to their forgiveness of sins. This new way of life transformed them in such a way that they were now willing to lay down their lives in order to hold on that new way.

One of my favorite passages from the Scriptures is the story of Paul and Silas in jail.

- About midnight, while Paul and Silas were praying and singing hymns to God as the prisoners listened, there was suddenly such a severe earthquake that the foundations of the jail shook; all the doors flew open, and the chains of all were pulled loose.
When the jailer woke up and saw the prison doors wide open, he drew his sword and was about to kill himself, thinking that the prisoners had escaped."

The story takes a stunning turn here. The guard is a most interesting subject here. Instead of suicide for letting his prisoners escape, the guard instantly becomes an accomplice, bringing Paul and Silas home to be fed and for his family to be baptized.

- But Paul shouted out in a loud voice, "Do no harm to yourself; we are all here." He asked for a light and rushed in and, trembling with fear, he fell down before Paul and Silas. Then he brought them out and said, "Sirs, what must I do to be saved?" And they said, "Believe in the Lord Jesus and you and your household will be saved." So they spoke the word of the Lord to him and to everyone in his house. He took them in at that hour of the night and bathed their wounds; then he and all his family were baptized at once. He brought them up into his house and pro-

vided a meal and with his household re-
joiced at having come to faith in
God." (Acts 16:26-34)

This is the perfect moment of grace, where everything is turned on its head, when the prison guard
moved from almost suicide itself to becoming a
disciple of Christ. That prison guard must have
instantaneously experienced the entire paradox
that the Spirit laid out for him that midnight.

Experiencing Grace Today

Throughout history, the church has witnessed
over and over again this rebirth process, and the
paradox contained within it. I think every missioner today understands that they are not bringing Christ to the culture they have visited, but
rather that Christ was already there, waiting for
the opportunity to touch the lives of the un-evan-
gelized with this wonderful paradox.

The most dramatic part of this paradox is that the
conversion of the lost soul doesn't just end with
the forgiveness of sins. It continues beyond to the
discovery of the dignity of the disciple of Christ
and the goodness inherent in that person. In a
clear way, that person is lifted to the point of experiencing the supernatural that God has placed
within them, but has hidden away for the day of
their conversion. In the end, we come to the

knowledge that this new life has been placed within us by God Himself from our very conception, perhaps even from all eternity. In the end, there are few words to describe the full heart of this paradox.

Why would the Father in heaven have bothered with us? Nothing within ourselves warrants any action on the part of God. The gifts we have received are far above anything we have done, and far contrast with the sinfulness with which we have desecrated God's creation.

And then, there is Christ's dying and rising. That moment far exceeds the forgiveness of sin that we were helpless to overcome, but climaxes in this new way, this new creation to which we have been invited. This invitation is not just for what lies beyond our deaths, but exists now, to be experienced in our daily lives in this world. In Christ, we meet the ultimate experience of the paradox: our sins forgiven, our lives transformed.

Always, if we look deeply enough, every celebration of Mass takes us to this point. Every time the Body and Blood of Christ is lifted up it is about this paradox. Even beyond that, we are taken to the actual moment that this happens, where Christ on the cross is giving Himself in a total act of humility and poverty, so that we might experience this paradox. Every time we receive Communion, we are brought to the sum of these mysteries.

Holding Both Parts of the Paradox

There is an additional dimension to this paradox in these contemporary times. One might think that if we lose the sense of our own sinfulness, we might still retain a sense of the new life in Christ that is the other part of the paradox. Somehow we assume we can do without the heavier emphasis on our own sinfulness, in order to more directly focus on the gifts and blessings that we have been given.

This is particularly poignant for our times. Over the past decades, Catholics have drifted further and further away from an awareness of our own deep roots in sinfulness. We easily believe that sin no longer exists. We like the warm fuzzies way better than the cold pricklies. In essence, the temptation of this age is to ignore the nature of our sins, yet try to hold on to the second half of the paradox, the gifts of grace. That attempt is destined to fail.

We try to hold on to the resurrection, seemingly without holding on at the same time to the cross. We hold on to the assumption that we are all good, even if we haven't lived as we ought to have. Our salvation is supposedly not a problem. Everybody is in, anyway, we think. We end up sanitizing the paradox, rather than owning it. This has been the legacy of the decades from the 1960's forward.

Both Moments Required

The fact of the matter is, that without the first part of the paradox, the awareness of our sinfulness, we also lose the other part of the paradox, the newness into which our conversion and baptism brings us. Instead, we thus end up in a kind of feel good, self-satisfaction. We easily assume that we are above the failures of existence, that there is no hell, and dying will simply move us into a well deserved state of fulfillment. Our neutral indifference will be sufficient to get us there.

So much for Lazarus at the gate, whom we never noticed! So much for our Holy week trips to the noted Mexican resorts or the cruise ships that we think we deserve! So much for choosing any alternative other than Mass to do on Sunday mornings!

On the contrary, the awareness of our sinfulness, of our unworthiness to stand before the Lord, remains the initial step to living completely in Christ. Only when we are awakened to the knowledge of our sinfulness will we be open to the discovery of what the call of Christ actually is for us. Only then, will we recognize that Christ is leading us day by day into the kingdom of God in this world. Then, the paradox will become explicit and astounding to our very depths, a double gift of both the healing of our past and the blessing of our present. This paradox alone can give us the complete picture of God's grace within us.

10. The Invisible

- Jesus said, "I came into this world for judgment, so that those who do not see might see, and those who do see might become blind."
 Some of the Pharisees who were with him heard this and said to him, "Surely we are not also blind, are we?" Jesus said to them, "If you were blind, you would have no sin; but now you are saying, 'We see,' so your sin remains."
 John 9.35-41

The Invisible Milky Way

For about five years, I lived in an area where you could barely see any stars in the sky, or even to see much of the Milky Way. I had been a Maryknoll Associate missioner in Korea for those five years, living in first in Seoul, a city of at least ten million, then in Songnam, with another two million. The night lights of the city usually obscured the presence of the Milky Way almost completely. If and when that didn't, the smog did.

Then, I returned to Southern Minnesota to become a pastor of a small, rural parish out where the Western prairie of the United States begins, the village of West Concord. The contrast couldn't have been any heavier!

I looked up at the sky on a summer night when I first began to reside in West Concord, and saw for the first time in five years, an endless array of stars, illuminating the night sky. These stars were accentuated by the Milky Way, a kind of silver ribbon winding its way through all the other, countless stars. Those uncountable stars, along with the Milky Way, punctuated the darkness from North to South and East to West. I had forgotten the beauty of the night stars, just because it was virtually invisible where I had been on mission.

What was visible in the nights of the Minnesota prairie was only a shadow in the orient, with most of the stars invisible because of both the city lights and because of the pollution of a very crowded urban area. I was stunned when I once more saw those stars in rural Minnesota that had been virtually invisible in the Korean city where I lived for those five years, first in Seoul, and then in Songnam City.

Indeed, after those five years I had forgotten the beauty and the wonder of the millions of stars that illuminate the nights of the prairie. I was saddened by the thought of how many cities, how many millions and millions of people around the world were denied the wonders of a starlit night, living as they were in a megapolis somewhere,

clouded over at night with such pollution, and
with city lights that were never extinguished.

An Analogy of the Secular Era

The invisibility of the stars in the cities of this era
is similar to grace in our postmodern times. Without the eyes of faith, those committed to this era
of the secular have no vision for grace. That gift of
grace, showered down upon our world, becomes
virtually invisible.

However, for us, as disciples of Christ, a rich and
beautiful array of grace rains upon us day by day.
In seeing with the eyes of faith, the kingdom of
God becomes visible to us. Central to this way of
seeing is the living presence of Christ. This presence of Christ is confirmed over and over by the
gift of the Eucharist.

Along with that, the effects of the grace of God's
love remains hidden and invisible to this era of the
secular. No one, without the eyes of faith, can see
the flow of constant gifts of grace that come like
the wind of the Holy Spirit. How similar to the invisibility of the stars is the effect of the secularism
of our times. To live without an awareness of the
grace that surrounds them, the world ends up
trapped in a horizontal, two-dimensional way of
seeing. There is no Christ present to them, no
grace that is poured out on them, no forgiveness
or rebirth. It is as if one were born into this world

but were never to see the stars in the night sky
above.

Grace Illuminates These Times

Let's take this issue of invisibility, this starless era
of the secular, and approach it from the standpoint of grace.

The gift of grace in our lives is the keystone to
what remains invisible to this era. Without the
keystone of grace, that is, the love of God sur-
rounding and completing us, everything remains
inaccessible. Everything spiritual then remains
locked up deep within us, or is just incomprehensible. Without this awareness of grace, the real
meaning and truth of our lives is simply absent.

The good news is that God's grace is incredibly
simple, available to whomever might seek it. The
presence of Jesus Christ comes to us wrapped in
the light of grace. He is risen, ready to walk with
us, unhidden to anyone with an open and repentant heart, open to anyone with a humble and sincere heart.

The central issue facing the 21st Century has to
do with the question of recognizing the presence
of Jesus Christ in this era. Everything else is pe-
ripheral, a waste of time as well. Ultimately, there
is no other issue except to recognize the profound
presence of Our Lord and Savior. Everything else
pales in comparison. Without this wondrous pres-

ence of Christ with us, it remains impossible to
sense the grace that, in fact, surrounds us. If
Christ is with us, we will be able to live our faith
completely in these troubled times, touched by the
presence of grace.

A Presence in a Climate of Invisibility

Never before has Jesus Christ been considered to
be so irrelevant to this world. Reduced to nothing
more than a man, who maybe lived 2000 years
ago before being murdered, He is assumed to be
gone and forgotten. The secular world cannot
even comprehend how it could be that we who are
Catholic actually think and believe that we have
the risen Christ with us on a daily basis. It is incomprehensible to these times, that Jesus Christ
might be guiding and directing our faith, walking
with us through temptations, reaching out to us in
our confusion and uncertainty.

This presence is so alien that this secular era cannot even imagine that it might be the truth. It
would be somewhat like a person living in some
megapolis, who has never even seen the Milky
Way or the star filled lights of night.

For us, as Catholic, once we have an awareness of
the presence of Christ, fed by the Eucharist, and
flooded with the gift of grace, we would not ever
choose its opposite. Never ever!

The postmodern world turns towards us and shakes its head, wondering how we could possibly be living in such a fantasy world. How could anyone be so naive? How could we ever hold that Christ is both alive and present to us. How could Christ Himself still be manifesting the wounds and brutality that had killed Him, but now in a glorified state? All that is incomprehensible. Of course, much of that blindness is self-inflicted, a chosen state of worldliness!

Thus, the contemporary era struggles along without something immensely beautiful, something seemingly absent, and invisible to them. What is invisible to them is like a star filled night out on the prairie for us. What they lack, and what we have is rich in meaning, showering us in hope.

Grace Before and After

There is a question that might occur at this point. Which comes first, the grace or the awareness of the presence of Christ with us? I suspect there is no answer to this question. I also suspect that grace both precedes and follows our yes to Christ. I think the Holy Spirit tips us into a sense of humility and simplicity. The Spirit Himself draws us over the edge into an awareness of our sins, and over the obstacles into the beginnings of conversion. Once that yes is made on our part, then, grace takes on a new and different dimension in our souls, and immediately leads us to an awareness that Christ is with us.

Grace, this special love of God for us, changes everything. Grace opens us up to see with the eyes of faith. Most often we are dumbstruck by what windows open up to us in the mystery of grace. It is beyond comprehension that the invisible becomes visible.

Grace opens us to Christ with us, stops us in our tracks, so that we would turn towards Christ, and allow Him lordship of our lives. We are then awakened to the truth and beauty that only Christ can reveal to us. Once these followup doses of grace touch us, there is a cascade of truths and values we never knew before, or could imagine but never possess. All of a sudden, something like billions of stars become visible, with Christ as a kind of milky way at the center.

In that moment, there is a flood of consequences to the presence of Christ with us. If Jesus Christ is real today: truth reappears. Morality now makes sense. Right and wrong are are clearer to us. We then know who we are, from where we have come, why we are here, and to where we are going. We know how to live, despite the challenges this secular era gives us. All that, is accessible to us now, because there is an overflowing of grace in our hearts and souls. We end up enlivened with an awareness of the presence of Christ in us!

All of a sudden, then, with the presence of Christ with us, guilt and sin takes on a new perspective. We have an awareness overwhelmed by the forgiveness open to us in a deeply personal way.

This modern world dare not take such a close look at the Christ, especially without an understanding of that forgiveness. Clearly his presence would have consequences that the 21st Century does not want to have to address. If Christ is the Lord of my life, my life's not my own, it is His! Therefore, He supposedly can't be, hence the apparent invisibility!

Yet, how close Christ is. How near and abounding is the grace with which Christ is surrounded, radiant and alive to anyone who would turn to him in humility and simplicity. Once again, the visible in the midst of the invisible!

As always the condition of this secular era means that there are thousands who might easily be brought to Christ. These are the ones that the Spirit will bring to us. This is a time to seek with all our hearts this gift of seeing with the eyes of faith. There are millions lost in the impenetrable darkness, supposedly illuminated by the bright lights of this age. The lights of this age exist to make the light of Christ invisible. Yet, the light of Christ and the grace of the love of God alone is what will define the darkness of this era for exactly what it is.

11. Weakness

- "Whoever wishes to come after me must deny himself, take up his cross, and follow me. For whoever wishes to save his life will lose it, but whoever loses his life for my sake and that of the gospel will save it. What profit is there for one to gain the whole world and forfeit his life? What could one give in exchange for his life?" Mark 8.34-37

The Cross in Our Lives

A key part of understanding grace in our lives is to understand the relationship of grace to our human weakness. Each of us seems to have some built in flaws, deep within our souls, seemingly mortal injuries in our very nature.

Often times we refer to these situations in our lives as having a cross to bear. To understand these crosses revealed in our weakness is to understand grace in our lives. Without a sense of the cross in our lives, we fail to turn to Christ in whom lies the gift of grace that we need so badly to deal with this inherent weakness.

Thus, our weakness, highlighted by our sense of the cross, becomes the key to reaching for the grace that comes from above. No one is immune from human weakness. Everyone somehow confronts this basic flaw of human life, whether from within or without. The secret within our crosses, then, is the grace that raises us above those weaknesses of our nature.

Wealth or status, youth or health are no protection in the long run. In fact, often those who seem protected from these challenges to our lives have forgotten that self protection is no protection at all. Instead, wealth or human security can end in an illusion that grace not be necessary, and that my security and status are enough to protect me from the endless variables that can give rise to the cross in us. Living in this world very quickly teaches us that there is nothing more illusionary than invulnerability.

Then when weakness and failure finally show themselves, there seems no grace to fall back upon, and no redeemer to whom to relate. Thus the tragedy of human life is doubled, with nowhere to turn in this world.

To boot, attempts to avoid our crosses often leads us even more deeply into the cross. As we struggle on our own, without the grace from above, the effects of our weakness and failures only intensify. As we see the secular character of this 21st century, we can only in sadness witness the resulting chaos that results from the experience of the cross separated from the realm of grace. This is the heart of the postmodern world, the secular era in which we live. Weakness and the cross dominate and enslave without grace.

This 21st century is becoming a prison of the horizontal, a death march with nothing transcendental to fall back on. In the loss of God's grace, the most vital cog of existence is absent. That missing piece is the Father's eternal love for us as his creation, and in the sending of his Son for our redemption.

Grace, the Pathway

Here is where our weakness steps in for us. Our weakness turns and awakens us to the potential that grace might have for us. Our failures bring us to seek out the hidden but present Christ who will especially walk with us in these matters.

All it takes for us to turn to this gift of grace is a dose of humility, a kind of simplicity, an awareness of our sins, and an openness that Our Father in heaven has placed within us.

Our flaws, our failures, and that inherent weakness that we have are so important to our conversion. All these things within our souls broadcast to whom and to what we have been designed to turn towards. The gift of grace waits patiently, beckoning us to abandon what will never work in this world, and to turn our hearts to what is from above.

The fact is, only grace, and grace alone, can provide us a pathway through the inherent weaknesses of our nature and character. Without this grace, we end up deeper and deeper into tragedy and chaos.

Note that grace does not remove the cross from our lives. Our weakness and failures persist, but this time with added resource of God's grace. The cross remains intrinsic to our fallen natures, to what Adam and Eve's actions gave us as a legacy. However, grace from above strengthens us in the exact experience of the cross. The presence of grace allows us to live in a way that transcends the horizontal, two dimensional format of the secular era. Grace consecrates our crosses. Grace lifts our failure to a new dimension. Our weaknesses turn us to the grace from above, helping us to discern how our weaknesses and grace go together.

Greater than Freedom from Desire

In my acquaintance with Buddhism from my days in the Orient, I came to understand a little of what Gautama Buddha preached his lifetime. The Buddha said that if we could rise above desire we could live out our days in a kind of peace and harmony. Desire itself was the enemy of peace of heart. The best life, supposedly, was freedom from desire.

The symbol of that truth was the precious stone, placed in forehead of every statue of the Buddha. Also, the one finger pointing upward in many of his statues, was to tell us the secret to the good life, that the absence of desire is the key to everything.

For us who are Catholic and Christian, that is not even much beyond the start of a more precious truth. When we open ourselves to Christ, yield our lives whole and entire to Him, the grace of the Holy Spirit reaches deeply within our souls. Turning to Christ starts us on a path that raises us up to a new level of existence that overwhelms the weakness and failure, even though the cross not be removed.

Buddha's solution, as good as it is, doesn't raise anyone to the level of the grace of God's love. God's grace reshapes our identity, our destiny, and our meaning to a new level. This is a level of our lives that we can't reach apart from the grace that is the overwhelming love of the Trinity for us.

We still carry our fallen nature, our sinfulness, our weaknesses and failures, yet we are made aware that Christ's presence is remaking us into his own image, making us one in Him. The initial passageway to grace is our sinfulness, our weaknesses and our failures. In short, the cross, unique to each of us turns us to the grace from above.

The cross itself is the secret of grace. No other religion or philosophy proclaims such a horizon or this kind of transcendence. There is nothing else in this world as breathtaking as this mystery of grace, and what it does to us. Grace, without Christ or Our Father in heaven, is forever blocked. However in Christ, that gateway yawns wide open.

Experience of the Priesthood and Religious Life

Weakness plays a significant role in God's call to someone entering or living in the priesthood or religious life. Usually we assume that a person might be called to the religious life because of the gifts that they have, that the Lord might utilize in proclaiming the kingdom of God. In other words, we sometimes think that God calls us because of our abilities and strengths.

However, I'd like to suggest that it is often in our weaknesses that God most calls us to serve Him. It is not how powerful or talented we might be that most opens us to God's grace from above. Rather, it is more often in our weaknesses whereby we turn from any self confidence to reach out to the grace from above. It is this grace which alone can empower us to live with the demands and difficulties of responding to God's call.

Often, our weaknesses are the secret in turning completely to Christ. Our weaknesses alone might bring us to yield finally to the grace that can help us rise above our broken and fragmented natures. Our weaknesses open the door to living by grace, in Christ alone.

We need a spirit of gratitude for our weaknesses and failures. This alone put us on the right track. What have we to say to the rest of humanity, except from our true knowledge of our own weaknesses? What have we to say to others, if we are unaware of being lifted above by the grace that surrounds our human natures?

The Experience of Love in Marriage

The same, I believe, is true for marriage and the family. In marriage, God's call to the couple is irrespective of how perfect their love for each other is, or what gifts they might bring to parenting. Every Sacrament of marriage contains the promise of grace in lieu of the weaknesses and crosses that the couple might bring to married life.

How many have gone into marriage, thinking that they need no help from above, believing that Christ was irrelevant to the success of a marriage. After all, "We are in love, and love alone is enough to give us power over our lives." The wedding can sometimes be a two dimensional, horizontal celebration, somehow missing the need for the presence of Christ and the grace from above to make that love most fruitful. No wonder vows are so easily broken in these times.

Unfortunately, love is one of the areas that becomes most difficult, given our human nature. In the absence of the presence of Christ with us, in a life style devoid of the belief of the need for God's grace, what is left of the realm of love? On the other hand, given the presence of Christ and the grace of the Holy Spirit, the couple has an array of gifts and tools above and beyond what Valentines Day proposes, or what a two dimensional set of vows promises.

The fact is, love is the most important piece in a marriage, but also the most fragile, given our human nature. In order for human love to be fulfilled, the theological piece of love must be there. That piece is the love from above, from Christ. Divine love, divine grace, flowing from Our Father in heaven, in Christ, is absolutely required for human love to become all that it could be.

How foolish it is to try to live without the presence of Christ. We need to be in possession of the gateway of grace, with an awareness of the extent of Our Father's heavenly love, and of the Spirit's outpouring of that grace. How could anyone pretend that they are capable of selfless love all on our own, apart from having even a limited sense of the cross of Christ in its promise of the gift of grace? We only have that capability tied to Christ Himself. Hence the importance of our prayer, our participation in the Eucharist, and in the cleansing by the Sacrament of Confession.

Weakness is a significant part of a successful marriage. Weakness makes the couple deeply aware of what it will take to protect the fragility of love. Grace from above leads to a spirit of forgiveness, to a sense of generosity, and to an openness to sacrifice. Weakness plus grace leads to nothing short of a true spirit of humility and poverty.

This is also the key to parenting, as well. Nothing in this era of the secular will be sufficient to bring parenting in marriage to this level of divine love. Indeed, the cross, coupled with grace, is intrinsic to human love and to the human family at its best.

This puts Catholic marriage in a unique position in this secular era. Nothing short of the frequent reception of Christ in all the Sacraments will suffice to infuse and radiate the divine nature of love. Grace in us lifts all of us to a new way of living, above and outside our weaknesses and our fallen natures. Our weaknesses do not go away in grace, they simply yield to the power that comes from above.

The gateway to love is blocked by the weakness of human nature. The only gateway to love that works is that of the presence of Christ with us, that opens us to the gifts of grace from above. Once we discover our weaknesses and the impossibility of overcoming them on our own, we are right at the point of turning to Christ. Christ alone is the one that pours out into our hearts grace from above, the grace that remakes us after his own image and likeness. Only in Christ will we

know who we are and how to truly love as we
ought. Thank God for all our weaknesses.

Always the Cross

The ownership of the cross, the one that is unique
to our individual lives, opens the gateway to the
grace of Jesus Christ. This openness enables Him
to take over our lives, to invest ourselves even
more deeply into the eternal life that is to come.

When there is a sense of the cross, with even a
simple understanding of the cross, we can come to
a sense of acceptance, and learn to see it with the
eyes of faith. In the cross, for us, there is always a
sense of expectation, that somehow out of this
cross, God's grace will blossom within our lives.

It matters little whether this cross arises out of
our weakness, or out of our failures, or out of our
built in flaws. What matters is the knowledge of
what is behind the experience of the cross, that
the grace of God's love will arise and be borne
somehow out of that most unlikely situation of the
cross within us. The deeper the contradictions in
our hearts, the greater the potential of grace in
that exact same place.

12. Martyrdom

- Blessed are they who are persecuted for the sake of righteousness, for theirs is the kingdom of heaven. Blessed are you when they insult you and persecute you and utter every kind of evil against you falsely because of me. Rejoice and be glad, for your reward will be great in heaven. Thus they persecuted the prophets who were before you.
Matthew 5:10-11

Saint Joseph Im

I suspect that martyrdom is the supreme level of the experience of grace that is possible in faith. Perhaps a story of one of the least known of Korean martyrs could illustrate the absolute power of grace.

In the early spring of 1984, Pope John Paul, now Saint John Paul, came to Seoul, Korea. During his visit there, he raised 103 Korean martyrs to the level of sainthood, the most prominent of which was Saint Andrew Kim Taeguon, the first native priest ordained in the Korean Catholic Church.

One of the least known of those 103 martyrs was a man who would be known in baptism as Joseph Im.

However, Saint Joseph had a strange connection to St. Andrew Kim Taeguon. Saint Joseph's son was the navigator on a boat bringing Saint Andrew up the coast of Korea. The boat was stopped and all on the boat were arrested under suspicion of being Catholic.

Next the authorities reached out to the families of those arrested to also arrest any family members from that boat's occupants that might also have become a part of this new, secret group that seemed to be spreading, especially among the poor and illiterate.

These Catholics threatened the ruling class that held power under the king. This Catholicism raised the dignity and level of the poor and uneducated to a kind of status equivalent to that of the ruling class in that kingdom.

In fact, there was a wide division between the educated and powerful and the so called peasant class, a division that this ruling class thought had to be maintained. This Catholicism, imported from the West by French missioners, thus needed to be stopped at any cost!

Arrested as Catholic

Thus it happened that this uneducated, poor man, Joseph, the father of one of the occupants of the boatload of arrested people, was also called to account, to make sure that he had not gone over to being a catholic.

However, as it turned out, Joseph, even though he knew nothing of what the catholics believed, decided upon his arrest that he too ought to be a catholic. His thinking was that, if it was important enough to be arrested under suspicion of being catholic, perhaps this even was enough, now with a new sense of dignity, that he could have a new identity, that of being catholic.

Thus, at that moment when he was arrested under suspicion of being catholic, he decided, then and there, to become a catholic. He decided his fate, while he was being hauled off to prison, the same prison where St. Andrew was being held.

When Joseph was called before the judge, the judge could see that Joseph was an uneducated, illiterate man, and bent over backwards to allow him a way to avoid being condemned as the others would be. The judge said, "You know nothing of being catholic, how could you be one?"

To which Joseph replied, saying, "Even a child knows simple things that are true, and I know now that God is my Father. So, I am a catholic."

Thus, Joseph was garroted with the others in the prison, for the crime of being catholic. Saint Andrew had instructed him further and baptized him while they were there together in prison. By the time of his martyrdom, he had a more complete understanding of what it meant to be a disciple of Jesus Christ.

As it was, Joseph knew only one third of the sign of the cross at the time of his trial. That was the extent of his faith knowledge, but it was enough in his mind to become fully a catholic. What could have possessed this ordinary man to become so convinced of the truth of the faith, that he would give up his life for it?

The Ultimate of Grace

The threshold of grace is never more apparent than at the moment of martyrdom. In fact, grace and martyrdom are a one, ultimate experience joined together in discipleship in Christ.

Always, grace transforms the person, who has been enveloped by that grace. In Saint Joseph's case, he was a part of a two part culture, born outside of the elite upper division. This elite consisted of all those relating in someway to the royalty of the kingdom of Korea. This elite were those who ranked highly in Confucian culture, who were well educated, and held both office and wealth. The culture was vertical. St. Joseph was at the bottom.

As a peasant, Joseph had no common ground with these elite. He was, in effect, a nobody, ignorant and uneducated, probably pretty much without reading and writing skills. He was disposable, and insignificant to those of the elite. How dare he exert himself, as one of dignity and worth. This Catholicism was making him somehow equal to those who had been ranked far above from birth, education and status.

While some of those elite had discovered the truth of Christianity, they were quickly ostracized and isolated as members of this new and uprooting belief in Jesus Christ. The root of this new religion had come from China, where some educated Koreans had discovered a Catholic catechism. This catechism had been authored by Fr. Matteo Ricci, a Jesuit priest who had spent more than twenty-five years living in China, and was instrumental in the beginnings of the Catholic Church in that country.

Why did this faith take root there both in China and in their neighbor, Korea? People paid a high price in Korea to be members, just as those in neighboring Japan and in distant Vietnam did. Ten thousand were martyred just in Korea, most in the 19th Century.

What could have possibly compelled such bravery, such determination on the part of the poor es-

pecially? What could have compelled such a dras-
tic step to be taken by the elite of that culture,
willing to go to such lengths that they would kill
in such numbers? What was it that these martyrs
found, and such murderers feared?

The Consequences of Grace

In the extremity of martyrdom, we can begin to
recognize the ultimate of the gift of grace in the
life of the Christian. In martyrdom, the awesome
transformation of grace highlights all the dimensions within the soul of the one who is experiencing martyrdom. This ultimate moment of grace is
a flood poured out from above, that could only
come from the Holy Spirit. Grace is never more in
focus than in these martyrs of our faith.

Let's break apart for a moment of what some of
the pieces of which this gift of grace is composed.
We know that, while we are not at the level of
those who suffered martyrdom, grace works the
same way within our lives, albeit less focused.
Perhaps the example of Saint Joseph's choice to
die for his newfound faith can give us insight into
our own experience of this gift of grace in our
souls.

Identity

Here in the 21st Century, in this time of such extreme individualism, this climate of self fulfillment, many are is search of their true identity. Unfortunately, in this two dimensional, horizontal era of the 21st Century, the search for identity is fruitless, frustrating and confusing.

There is, in fact, no identity, without Christ, other than a kind of "self creation" that one might attain today, a lifting up of one's self by the boot straps. There is nothing intrinsic to the life of the secular era other than what a person might invent. Identity has no foundation, no roots, no substance in these times without Jesus Christ.

There is a reason why such an emptiness of identity is so today. This is because in the end our true identity can be achieved only in relationship to Christ Jesus and to His Heavenly Father. Apart of this awareness of us being drawn in its substance and heart from above, there is no identity truly possible. Identity without Christ is a kind of cats cradle, a momentary and fickle illusion, disconnected from anything that God has put within us. Thus, who we are remains absolutely lost, if all we have is the secular era!

Truly, only in Christ will we ever know who we are. Only in the awareness that God is our Father will we have the identity that matches up exactly with what is imprinted in our nature. That identity resides in our souls locked up, hidden as a result of Adam and Eve's fall. Our identity emerges only completely when we are somehow in relation to Christ, who then shows us His Father. Who we are ultimately cannot be determined except in relationship with Christ and His Father. Identity somehow not joined to Christ remains an illusion, a cipher, undefinable.

In Saint Joseph Im we can recognize that when he was arrested, he immediately knew a part of himself that was his latent identity, hidden away, waiting for that moment. This identity, this Christian dimension of his soul and heart immediately emerged, giving him the courage and determination that nothing more than this newly found faith was worth living for. This is the gateway that grace opens in our lives, stunning us by where it leads us. In that moment, we know exactly who we are. We realize that we have been defined from all eternity in the plan of God, with a Christian identity now open before us.

Dignity

Dignity today is a willow-the-wisp of our times. Perhaps it has always been that way. However, it is heightened in these times, filled with the "haves" and the "have nots." In the desperation to discover our dignity in the midst of all this emptiness, it is reduced to a competition.

Reputations hang by a thread in this era of tribalism and social media. The worth of an individual is a non-entity today in public life. To boot, it appears today that the dignity of the individual grows progressively less important. Everyone and everything is fair game. Attack and humiliation substitute for dialogue. There is no such thing as reconciliation, rebirth or forgiveness.

Perhaps this assumption of lack of worth of every individual is fostered by the climate of abortion. If an unborn has no worth, why would anyone already born have any, except if it was self created. Everyone is simply expendable. Also, the climate of sexual freedom suggests the non-worth of every individual dealing with such misuse of their nature. Sexual abuse, at every level so existent today, cries out in condemnation about the absence of dignity and worth.

Not only in our times, but throughout history, the intrinsic dignity of the individual could never be assumed. Only in the very essence of Christianity could the intrinsic dignity and worth of the person be correctly understood. This was how Christianity stunned the Roman Empire, unveiling a new, theological sense of human dignity.

However, in our times, why can't we hold to that same sense of dignity and worth of the person? Perhaps this loss of dignity today comes from a culture that has lost its connection to the Lord above.

If there would be no god, would not humanity be free of any responsibility to respect and value every person alive, even of themselves? If every person conceived or born has come from above, how could we not treasure every single person we come in contact with. If we finally know who we are because we have seen the love of the Father in sacrificing his Son on the cross, how could we fail to turn to our brothers and sisters with the deepest respect. Always God's love must be the engine of our own love.

The fact is, we come to this point of dignity only in the grace from above. Grace remains the gateway to human dignity. Grace has only been fully revealed in the sacrifice of Christ on the cross, and what it means for every human being.

In Christ's dying on the cross, it appears on the surface that he was completely destroyed in his dignity and identity. No one could have experienced the descent and destruction that Jesus Christ endured, falling all the way from divinity to the immeasurable humiliation of the cross. His humanity was paper thin at that moment of dying on the cross. It couldn't have been less.

However, we know that in that moment he reached a dignity beyond all of creation, above all that is human, in total love for us and for his Father in heaven. Jesus redefined dignity in his total gift of self, Body and Blood, in his once for all sacrifice.

In our celebration of the Eucharist, we know that we are brought to that precise moment of Christ's gift of Himself to the Father. The Mass, then, redefines the meaning of dignity, because we know we are included in Christ's offering to the Father. Each person, receiving Communion, can begin to sense this new, inherent dignity that grace bestows.

Grace, then, is intrinsic to the celebration of the Eucharist, redefining everything human as sacred and holy. Grace, at that moment, touches each of us. In the Eucharist, Christ Himself reminds us of our own intrinsic worth and dignity. Thus, we know who we are, what our worth is, and how we are to relate to one another.

Saint Joseph Im must have immediately sensed this transformation as he was being walked to prison and his death. Until that moment, he had been this worthless nobody, whose life could be discarded at any moment. However, in an instant, it seems, he discovered a new dignity, a new worth, that only could have come from above. He found himself with a new dignity given him by the Spirit, awakening him to a destiny and value heretofore hidden deep within his soul. It is no wonder that he made this decision, despite the consequences to which it would lead.

Anchored

Grace anchors us in the kingdom of God. Grace gives us the certainty of hope, even in trying and fragmented times. There is no question about how important it is to be anchored somewhere, somehow in these times in this postmodern world.

In this era of the secular, one of its traits is that now existence connects to nothing. There is no anchor anywhere in the secular. This is one of the tragedies of our times that life is so rooted in nothing. It seems as if no resource is certain or solid in the culture of these times.

This nothingness, this sense of being unrooted anywhere is the result the culture having separated itself from anything from above. These times, without God, without Christ and without the Holy Spirit, are a frightening scenario. This troublesome scenario has been building slowly over the past centuries, and has been accelerating in the last decades.

The case made today by the media, that the Catholic Church is falling apart, that everyone is leaving the church, is an inverted concern to which our times might need to take a look. The ultimate question, that trumps these assumptions by our media, is the concern of a culture that has no anchor, that is connected nowhere to anything. The cost to the individual is immense, whoever now has no connection to anything but the internet, or to whichever way the wind is blowing in tribalism. These times are marked by the uproar, the identity politics, and the chaos of where all that might lead.

It is not the church that is collapsing. It is the godless culture in our midst!

For us as catholics, we have our anchor. The anchor is Jesus Christ, who alone orients and stabilizes what we are and how we are to live. In that presence of Christ with us, both in the Eucharist and in prayer, we know a new reality, knowable only in grace, grounded in the love of God for us, who was willing to pay any price to bring about our salvation. Indeed our anchor, our hope is rock solid.

This is how Saint Joseph Im could make his decision. This was how clear it was to him. He had the power of grace in him, that gave him an anchor from above, and the sure-footedness that protected him on his journey to martyrdom.

Awakened

Clearly, in grace there is an awakening. This awakening jars the convert to the new reality in which they have been immersed. Person after person, in relating their experience of conversion can testify to this awakening.

In addition, the presence of grace keeps this awakening alive not only at the beginning, but during the entire lifetime. The grace is a river that continues to flow throughout our lives of faith. There is no end to the surprise.

The initial forgiveness that is experienced clears up the past sins and the failures. None of such a past needed to have been erased by the will of the person. The person who has found Jesus Christ, though, ends up lifted in the grace that flows from above in baptism. This experience of grace continues to flow within the soul. The experience of suffering, that is always a part of our existence, is given a meaning and a spirit of endurance, teaching us that there is even a sacred realm in that.

Always there is this surprise. Grace and surprise go together. Grace overwhelms our awareness, reminds us that where we have ended up today has no explanation other than God's love from above.

Perhaps this is the most remarkable part of grace, not a once in a lifetime, but is a continuing presence of the risen Christ with us, taking us where we had never expected to go. We find ourselves stunned by the goodness and healing that happens, again and again.

Imagine the awakening that Joseph Im experienced, where it took him in his life, to what it led him. It is as if one day Joseph was transformed from one creature to a new one. He had to have awakened to exactly what that grace from above was. It must have taken his breath away, even as it led him to the sacrifice of his breath here in this world!

13. The Rock

- Everyone who listens to these words of mine and acts on them will be like a wise man who built his house on rock. The rain fell, the floods came, and the winds blew and buffeted the house. But it did not collapse; it had been set solidly on rock. (Matthew 7:24-25)

Playing Chess, Lessons Learned

A long time ago, when I was in high school, with a school with a faculty of mainly Franciscan Sisters and diocesan priests, one of the hidden gifts to some of us was our school custodian. Named Raul Xavier, he was a refugee from China, probably from the time that Communism and Mao took over in the late 1940's.

For some reason a group of us students had picked up the habit of playing chess in the band room, whenever we had an open period or after dismissal. Raul, the custodian, often joined us, and surprised us with the extent of his knowledge of the game of chess.

As such, our custodian became a kind of adjunct teacher, behind the scenes, and I think, unknown to the school itself. Raul taught us a great deal about the game of chess, as well as to the process of thought behind it. He was good enough that he would only play for a draw, rather than to win against us. Or maybe, we were bad enough that he could easily play for a draw. Whichever! After each game, he would show us new moves, ways in which the game left opportunities to win or lose.

Strangely enough, even among that excellent faculty, our custodian was one of those who was most memorable. Beyond the chess, he talked with us about his experiences in China growing up, experiences that he had.

In our times in school, we were lost in the hinterland of the 1950's America, about as far away from anywhere as you could get, in southern Minnesota. We were without the remotest knowledge of the world beyond.

A Parable from an Experience

I remember one of those moments that Raul had taught us. It seemed that once he had been caught in a flood, in one of the major rivers of China, and was swept away by the current. He told us that he struggled and struggled, swimming as best he could against the current until he ran out of energy. He said that finally he gave up and quit trying to save himself.

At that point he let himself start to sink. Surprisingly, he found that he had been struggling to swim in water about three to four feet deep, and that as he let his legs down he found he could stand, and walk towards the shore. He realized, he said, that he had been in water no deeper than that for almost the whole time, for possibly a mile or more, as he put it. How close to drowning he said he came, in just three to four feet of water!

Finding Our Footing

What a marvelous parable for our times! After all those years, I look back and find his story strangely revealing. Here we are swept away, as it were, by the secularism of contemporary times, by this junkyard of broken meaning. Undoubtedly the secularism of our times is a kind of wasteland of hope, or a shipwreck of morality. We are clearly caught up in this progressively deteriorating culture of postmodern humanity.

How often we try to swim against it, as if we were left on our own! How often we exhaust our energy struggling against something that we simply don't understand, against an enemy who seems the stronger. Often we are left exhausted, partially defeated these days by what has happened to morality, to the family, and to the kind of innocence we experienced growing up. Often we feel as if we are losing all that we hold precious in these contemporary times.

Yet, we have solid footing just below the surface of these times. That solid footing is the presence of the risen Christ in our midst, and the grace that his presence showers upon us. That presence manifests itself most in the mystery of the Mass, in the strength of the Eucharist.

In fact, we have everything we need to deal with these present times. In addition, our rescue is right here for us, within reach! Why do we so often try to do it on our own, trying to swim when we could just stand firmly on the presence of Christ, in the love of the Father, and in the gifts of the Spirit?

Behold, I am with You Always

The very last line of the Gospel according to Matthew ends with the words: "And behold, I am with you always, until the end of the age." Here we are, so frightened that we are losing the grip of all that we value, so worried that this inverted alternative universe of Satan is going to overwhelm us.

What we don't remember is the very essence of what Jesus Christ came to teach us, and to do for us by dying on the cross. He shares the same with us in his gift of the Eucharist. His presence is a solid rock on which we can depend. We are to remember the spiritual power that flows from his side on the cross, the blood and the water.

The defeat of Satan's alternative universe has already been determined, and in fact, has happened. We simply forget who it was that began our total redemption, and that has already proscribed the final curtain yet to come, Jesus Christ.

Clearly, Christ came to transform our weakened and fragile human nature and character into an eternal way of living. In addition, he came to teach us that all the power resides in his hands, and that all the love necessary for us in these times flows from the Holy Spirit. In Christ alone is the revelation that Our Father in heaven is waiting patiently for us to give ourselves totally to his Son. Once we acknowledge this truth, we can turn and say, "What was it that we were so afraid of, that we were so frightened of?"

Suffering in the Secular Era

I suspect that more often than not, it is suffering that we fail to understand, and that we recoil from. We have somehow gotten the notion that if we are suffering in this world in these times, it is a sign of defeat for us. Simply in any suffering in these times we assume that this world is winning against us. That's understandable, given the context in which we live, in this postmodern era. This tendency makes us flee anything like suffering, as if it were the absolute worst thing that could ever happen.

On the contrary, any suffering that we endure, because of our faith in Jesus Christ, would be for us the maximum revelation of the power of grace in our lives. Outside of martyrdom itself, there isn't anything where the power of grace is more visible than in our suffering. There is nothing where there is a more solid foundation for us spiritually. Grace is at its greatest potential in our lives in our suffering. Or, to put it another way, the ultimate revelation of grace in our world can be our attitude towards whatever suffering befalls us.

Granted, we need not go looking for suffering. We don't need to go find more suffering; it just comes to all of us. Suffering is part of the essence of human life.

The critical juncture in our suffering is whether we have this solid connection to Christ in our hearts at the time. Thus, we can endure whatever lands on our doorsteps. God's grace will always and forever be sufficient to us, and will be supremely visible to us in our hardest and saddest moments. This knowledge will free us from having to twist our morality or compromise our values to accommodate what this era would attempt to force on us.

This inverted alternative universe of Satan is an illusion, a house of cards, a poorly constructed magic trick. This illusion fades into nothingness before the presence, the real presence of Jesus Christ in our midst. In Christ we need not flee our suffering. Why would anyone choose such an illusion as an alternative to Christ's grace? Why would we swim in desperation against drowning in these time, when all we have to do is stand on the solid ground of the presence of Christ?

Swimming in this Era

We are inundated with a media that can't get enough of secularism, that so seeks this postmodern environment. In the face of such worldly wealth or in identity politics, easily we begin to believe that these times are inevitable. We end up thinking that this era will somehow produce a kind of synchronized, seamless coherence, one that was somehow lacking in the past or in our faith. This era seems to promise a finely tuned, integrated world that could only come from the hands of modern science.

On the other hand, there is no heart to this postmodern world. There is no direction to it. The postmodern world starts from nowhere, is pointed nowhere, and doesn't know why it is here. Truth and goodness are endlessly variable in this postmodern context.

This is the era of the disconnected. In this era we easily become fugitives fleeing any kind of suffering. In that flight, we miss the riches of grace that would flow from offering our life and our days to Christ. We would miss that to which Christ Himself might be deeply calling us. We could walk with Christ, rather than swim alone.

Grace hidden within our Hearts

All of this secular system prevails in our minds because we, as Catholic and Christian, simply forget what it is that Our Father in heaven has prepared and hidden deep within our souls. Our true freedom can only come from our heartfelt connection to Christ. It can never come from how the times has imprisoned us, like swimmers in a flood. Again, we don't have to swim, we can stand, our feet on solid ground, in Christ.

Think of it this way: our Father in heaven has placed within us pieces of the supernatural, some of those things that Adam and Eve lost in their choice of the fruit from the tree of knowledge at the center of the garden. These pieces remain locked within us, hidden away, deeply imprinted within our souls, awaiting the moment when God can restore them in action within our lives. When we have Christ in us, these gifts emerge. We need not swim then, but can stand against the current.

We, however, in our state of original sin, easily think that by our own nature we can reach our potential, become the persons we want to be, and conquer everything in this world. How quickly it changes. There is nothing more scary in this secular era than to find out that this world is way beyond our own control, and that everything, even the world itself, all by itself, is destined to fail.

No question that these times leave us with much to worry about: climate change, vectors of new unheard of diseases, uncontrollable guns, drugs, the total collapse of the economy. The list is endless, and the further the century goes, the more stories and predictions there seem to be. How can anyone find a foothold in the flood of the 21st Century?

Grace and the Rock

What is it that we can find to stand upon, rather than swim endlessly and hopelessly alone in the way that this Century appears to require? The fact is, our human nature depends on grace from above, and that Christ Himself is the rock on which we can stand. Him alone! In Christ grace gives us solid ground; we don't have to swim on our own, we have the ground of grace in which we can walk and not be exhausted from the flood around us.

Of course, we know that grace will not remove the evil of these times, or that they will eliminate suffering and loss for us. Grace does not fix our world, but brings us to live for the kingdom of God, at a new level of morality and faith, despite the consequences of these times.

In addition, grace gives us the power to live for the truth of the Gospel, to stand firmly in the knowledge of right and wrong, without deviating from what the Gospel calls us to in purity and honesty. Grace moves us to turn from the wandering and desperation of this era. Grace allows us to live plain and simple lives, without compromise or hesitation, knowing exactly who we are and what we are about. In all this, God's grace will trump any suffering, any sacrifice that might be asked of us. In Christ, all is possible. In all of this, we can live out our faith in Christ Jesus, despite the consequences of this horizontal, two dimensional world,.

14. Tragedy

- I have been crucified with Christ; yet I
  live, no longer I, but Christ lives in me; in-
  sofar as I now live in the flesh, I live by
  faith in the Son of God who has loved me
  and given himself up for me.
  Gal. 2.19-20

The Car Seat

Some forty to fifty years ago there was a kind of
car seat for small children. This kind of car seat,
actually quite dangerous, hung over the back of
the front passenger seat. The child then was facing the front in the passenger seat, with legs dan-
gling above the passenger seat.

Often the child had its own little white, plastic
steering wheel attached to the car seat. This steering wheel was, of course, connected to nothing.
However, the child could pretend somehow that
he or she could steer.

Thus, as the car, let's say a 1957 chevy (like my
very first car ever), travelled down the street, and
there was another car coming towards them. The
child could fantasize that by turning that plastic
steering wheel quickly to the right, it was going to
prevent an accident. It was connected to nothing,

but always the car turned to avoid the oncoming vehicle, leaving the child with the illusion that their action might have been what prevented catastrophe.

Again, there's a tree off to the right that the car is approaching, and it would be a bad thing to hit. The child turns the plastic steering wheel to the left as fast as he can, and slowly the car turns to avoid hitting that tree. The plastic steering wheel is again connected to nothing, but leaves the child to imagine that his turning that wheel was maybe what prevented the problem. His father, of course, had control of the other wheel, the real one on the left side!

The Little Plastic Steering Wheel

The tragedy of the 21st Century is symbolized by that little plastic steering wheel. It's connected to nothing! It's all illusion in this time that we are in control. At the end of the day, we think we did it all. In fact, it has been a progressive, delusional journey for our culture. The secular climate now takes credit for all the successes over the past 60 to 70 years, that it all has been in our hands. This age thinks we were the ones who did all the good, achieved all the success. We did it!

We are certain that all this progress until now has been by our own efforts. In addition, we easily think we will have the ability to make the progress continue right through the rest of the 21st century. With our little plastic steering wheel, we do it all. Nothing can stop us.

The only problem is, our steering wheel is connected to nothing, not anything at all. This little white steering wheel by which we think we are steering this postmodern century has no connection to anything but ourselves. So here we are, in the 21st century, alone in the universe, like a child in a dangerous car seat, trapped on a planet that seems to be overheating in climate change. There we are, adrift in a culture that has lost any coherent sense of meaning. All we have to hold on to is this little white plastic steering wheel, connected to nothing.

Again, there we are, with suicides occurring more and more numerously, and there's nothing but this little plastic steering wheel in our hands. Something seems missing, and we wonder what that is.

Once more, the number of massacres with the use of guns just keeps expanding in some mysterious way. Again, there is nothing but that little white steering wheel to turn us away from it or to explain it all. When things become this violent in a culture, something seems missing. What could that be?

In addition, there is the opioid/heroin/cocaine epidemic, coupled with the growth of sexually transmitted diseases across the culture, and there is nothing to stop it all, except that little plastic steering wheel, connected to nothing. What is it that seems so missing in our lives that could prevent such a situation of helplessness?

Finally, there is the ever expanding gap between those with wealth and success, and the rest of the country that is struggling without assets, without proper insurance, without any safety net to get beyond this month. The whole country seems to have nothing but that little plastic steering wheel, totally useless to save us from a fiscal catastrophe. No wonder there is so much deep seated fear in people's lives today!

What's Missing?

How did it come to this in our country? What's missing? The truth is that we have decided that we are on our own, that we need neither God above, nor Christ present, because we are the center. We determine the future. We get to set the parameters. We can do it all. Our hands are on the steering wheel, and we can control it all.

This time of the secular, in the postmodernism of the 21st Century seems on the surface to have its act together, marshaling science, the media, popular psychology and sociology as a coherent body of absolute truth. This culture presents itself as now superior to any of the previous centuries, free of the enchantment and ignorant practices and beliefs of the past times. Finally, a time of complete rationality and intelligence!

The Open Gateway

We truly need a sense of compassion and prayer for this 21st Century. These times would have a massive task to shift from an extreme of the secular in order to return to the multidimensional, enchanted, transcendental realm of the sacred. Talk about a potential era of evangelization such as the world has never seen. Such would require a 180 degree shift, an absolute transformation like from a zero to infinity!

The potential for conversion, faith and even martyrdom will be astounding, like nothing seen since the days of Nero and the Roman Empire.

The gateway to this sacred realm is through the grace of Jesus Christ. Only in coming to know Christ do we reach the point of accessing the realm of the kingdom of God. Without the presence of Christ with us, all that is left is this world is a disenchanted blue planet, connected to nothing, coming from nowhere, going nowhere. So far as the postmodern world is concerned, there is no presence of Christ, and as a result there is, again, only this little white plastic steering wheel connected to nothing. Thus, the average disenchanted person has nowhere to turn, knowing nothing of Christ, that he might exist, that he might open doors to a different reality. Hope is a fugitive in the postmodern world, unless, of course, you come to know Jesus Christ in your heart!

This does not mean in any sense that the Spirit will not work with these victims of secularism. Indeed, the possibilities of conversion are infinite. If we who are Catholic understand who we are, and live our commitment to Christ to the full, we will simply be unlabeled evangelizers to this postmodern realm. We will be touching people wherever we are, raising new questions, opening new doors. There is great potential here, given the flaws and corruption inherent within the postmodern world, and despite the flawed humanity of us who are Church.

Grace in this Context

While I have underlined this era with considerable detail, there is also the presence of the grace of God. In the presence of grace in these times there is a truth to be considered, that the worse off things become, the more grace makes its appearance. In fact, like in the cross of Christ itself, the greater the defeat appears, the nearer the victory is.

Just when Satan will think that he has finally overcome things, that is exactly the moment when Christ's victory will shine for us. Where the substance of grace is only a little bit of salt, just the merest touch of yeast, or the smallest of mustard seeds, we will understand the nearness of Christ's victory on the cross for today's problems. A single candle gives a powerful light in total darkness.

Our understanding of the 21st Century, however, is absolutely critical. The more we understand the postmodern world, the more firmly we will take hold of our Catholic faith. The more we can address our own faith in Jesus Christ, then, the more this shipwreck of morality in the postmodern world will stand out.

The presence of God's love, especially in these times, will lead many away from the inverted alternative universe of Satan, and into the arms of Christ which can envelope us completely and safely in this era of denial. Grace has the power to unite us to the one who steers the final journey of all history, Our Father in heaven.

Imagine the depth of conversion that will be possible, as this disconnected, fragmenting world reaches its nadir. Imagine the awakening that will be possible for any person who possesses an open heart, a repentant conscience, or a humble spirit in this postmodern world.

Such a one will be able to navigate through every aspect of this double challenge, finally arriving at the truth of these times. Many of the victims of this secularism will ultimately be surprised to the max, that there is indeed a redeemer, that there is a pathway open to him or her. I believe that, despite their past, any will be welcomed into this realm of the sacred that, before, they had denied, and could never have imagined existed.

As always, the Eucharist

As always, the Mass stands as the pinnacle of this enchanted, transcendental realm. The Mass is the deepest point where we connect to all that is redemptive, to everything that gives meaning and purpose to our condition. The Eucharist opens a threshold of hope available nowhere else. The Eucharist is the absolute contradiction to the spirit of this postmodern world. It is the opposite of that little white steering wheel.

Thus, the ground zero for the postmodern Catholic remains this gentle, reflective celebration of the presence of Christ with us, the Mass and the Eucharist. This training ground will lead us into a spirit of evangelization, one that will simply be the presence of the risen Christ and the Holy Spirit. This simple, often hidden gift of the Eucharist will be able to give us the rock solid foundation that no secular era can stand against. In all of this, the community of the Church, with us united as one, in grace, will mushroom exponentially into the Church united as never before.

The fact of the matter is, the secularism of the 21st Century is simply not the overpowering force that it thinks it is, or even what many who are

Catholic might fear. This secular era is flawed to a huge degree. This postmodern secular era is a moth eaten contradiction, a rust filled misadventure, incapable of the truth. It will be known as an era searching aimlessly for some sort of goodness and oneness, absent to all but those who turn to Christ.

In the end, there we are, in weakness, but with the power of the risen Christ. His presence will be manifested time and time again in our celebration of the Eucharist. There we are, united in heart and soul with Christ our Savior, with the love of Our Father in heaven and with the presence of the Holy Spirit. There we are, participants and witnesses standing at the very gateway of grace from above.

15. Dust to Grace

-   This different kind of creature (man) has
    that "unstable ontological constitution"
    which makes it at once something greater
    and something less than itself. Hence that
    kind of dislocation, that mysterious lame-
    ness, due not merely to sin, but primarily
    and more fundamentally to being a crea-
    ture made out of nothing which, astound-
    ingly, touches God. "Like God in its mind."
    At once, and inextricably both "nothing"
    and "image."
    (Henri de Lubac)

Humanity without Grace

What an odd creature humanity is, this combination of dust and grace. We all know the dust portion of ourselves. It's where we end up in death, at
least with our bodies. We also remember the Genesis narrative of our creation:

-   "Then the LORD God formed the man
    out of the dust of the ground and blew into
    his nostrils the breath of life, and the man

became a living being."
(Genesis 2:7)

When God found what Adam and Eve had done, after their encounter with the snake, He told them:

-   "Cursed is the ground because of you! In toil you shall eat its yield all the days of your life. Thorns and thistles it shall bear for you, and you shall eat the grass of the field. By the sweat of your brow you shall eat bread, Until you return to the ground, from which you were taken; For you are dust, and to dust you shall return." (Genesis 3:18-19)

Thus, the trouble all emerged with the story of Adam and Eve. By their decision to become like gods, they ended up without grace, left with only the dust gathered and arranged by God. They were without the supernatural gifts from above, the only thing that would have made them or us whole and complete. This is a story of a two part puzzle where one part is missing, the result of what we call, "original sin."

Just Out of Reach

The thing is, even without the ability to attain a whole and complete life, humanity can still identify what that life could be. We want that whole and complete life, we can see it, but it remains just out of our reach. We grab for that wholeness, but end up grabbing any one piece, which in the end corrupts in our hands.

The absence of this grace is a huge problem for all of humanity, left wandering about the planet and throughout time with something missing, sometimes knowing what it might be, but most often not. At other times, we cannot grasp why we are, such as we are, just orphans and wanderers. This "grace" part of ourselves is something intrinsic to us, without which our identity flounders, our meaning fragments, and our tranquility trembles with uncertainty. We can see that there ought to be some sort of grace, but it appears inaccessible, at least by our own power.

At the same time, God's part in this story could be described in similar terms. Perhaps we could describe Our Father in heaven as a brokenhearted God. I know, strictly speaking, that broken heartedness is not an attribute of God to which we are accustomed.

Yet, why would Our Father in heaven not have some sense similar to a broken heart. We are his creation. From the very beginning he called us to be one with Him, and we have massively failed that call. If Christ wept over Jerusalem, if he felt that way about Lazarus' death, we could imagine Our Father in heaven, as it were, crushed and astounded by what has happened to the whole of his creation.

The Simplicity of God's Grace

Grace is such a simple thing. It is the love of God for us, personalized in the three persons of the Trinity, the Father, the Son and the Spirit. This love of God, without its presence manifested in our souls, is as ephemeral as the fog, a kind of mist that we can't quite see.

In one way, this absence of this key part of our humanity is a great, great tragedy. Our humanity is trapped in a pit, unable to escape from on our own, denying the very grace we need to escape. The way back to what existed before with Adam and Eve seems unattainable in any human way.

In the present context, of a world gone secular, Our Father in heaven cannot but be portrayed in some sense as a kind of victim of this present world, betrayed, abandoned, or assumed not to have even existed. That tragedy is doubled over, because humanity, in many ways lacks even the remotest openness to God. This postmodern world is a junkyard of a shattered humanity, seeking to go on without the least modicum of respect about our origin or our destiny. Put another way, we were intended to be a combination of dust and grace. Without the grace, we are indeed, somehow, just the dust.

The Rest of this Story

But wait, there is more to this story. The piece that has been missing, the grace, has been made available again. Surprisingly, the way back to that grace has been opened up for us in Christ. The Father sent his Son to forge a pathway back to what we were supposed to have been from the beginning, doing it in such a way as to trick Satan.

Satan, thinking murder would solve the problem of the Messiah's presence, tripped and stumbled over the non-violence and humility, the utter simplicity of Jesus Christ, giving Himself in perfect love to his Father in heaven for the sake of his children. Satan had thought that death would be a trap, but it turned out to be the doorway.

I suspect that the cross of Christ was God's plan from the very beginning. It was not plan "B." Christ's coming was planned before even our creation, before even the fall of Adam and Eve. Most likely, God's plan was always a two step plan, first with creation, then with incarnation and redemption. This plan now reaches all the way to the Eucharist and eternal life.

Perhaps, without this new step there would be no clear awareness to what God had planned from the beginning for us. Without it, we would never have know the extent of love that the Father has for us. God's plan included the completion of the incarnation and redemption from the very beginning, and that the grace would exist definitively in our midst. This grace then would able to be found and owned by the very ones who proved themselves unworthy and undeserving of that grace.

Nothing could possibly be a more beautiful story, with the Father reaching down to bring us home in his very Son. The incarnation of Jesus and the redemption by his death on the cross highlights and lifts our awareness to the extent of God's love, way beyond that of those initial days of Adam and Eve. We have learned that the love for us, the love of the Father and the Son together in the Spirit, is astronomically beyond what we can fully comprehend. Thus the Exsultet, the ancient hymn of the liturgy of Easter Vigil, proclaims: "O happy fault."

The Extent of God's Grace

It took the crucifixion and the death of his Son for the complete restoration of grace in our world. Only then do we learn the extent to which the Father was willing to go for us. Only then do we appreciate the extent of his love. Only then do we understand why He sent his Son. Only then do we have the ability to fully grasp the gift that has been given to us by his Son. Only then does love get redefined as absolute and perfect. Only then will we find the power of this latent gift of grace that flows within us. Only then would the Eucharist flow from the cross all the way into this 21st Century.

Thus we have this strange and bizarre situation in this postmodern world. The more the grace of God exists in our midst, the more this secular realm saturates itself with the denial, disregard and rejection of that very grace. Thus, the opposition to divine grace permeates the everyday life of those who should be open to the love of Christ and his Father. The more the grace, the greater the flight from it. The more the chaos of this time, the tighter humanity holds on to its estrangement from Christ. The more the dust of self divination defines who humanity is, the more invisible the grace of God's love remains in their lives.

The Reservoir of Grace

The curious thing is that this reservoir of grace for each of us is not stored up in some extra-universe of non-being. No, I believe the reservoir of grace lies hidden deeply within each of us, locked up, so to speak, latent and hidden there for the day when it could be revealed.

I suspect that God simply hid this grace deep in our souls, to await the time when it could emerge.

He buried the grace in our dust. Just as God anticipated the redemption in the creation, so also within us, He buried the gift of grace for that day when it could emerge to transform our lives. When we become aware of this emerging gift of grace, this action stuns us completely!

I believe that this hiddenness of God's grace within us is one of the most surprising gifts on God's part to us. That gift sits there and waits within us, for us to awaken from a self centered life. It waits there for us to grow weary of a broken and chaotic life of materialism and hedonism. Grace patiently awaits for us to address for the first time the hidden presence of Jesus Christ.

A Subtle Plan of Love

When that awakening finally happens, we are overwhelmed by the revelation of what our lives really mean, how our life changes, what we now understand about both ourselves and this world in which we live. We are made speechless by the forgiveness, humbled by what has happened.

When this grace awakens us, we are often somewhat afraid because, in grace, we are now entering a realm we never knew existed within us.

At the same time, we can't get enough of this incredible dimension of the love of God and Christ for us. We almost always fail to absorb it all. Everyday is a surprise for the one who finally turns to Jesus Christ. Grace ends up being that reality for which we cannot find words.

This experience is virtually beyond description in many ways. Even though we can't stop thinking about it, we can't even share the most of it. It is too sacred. It is a once in a lifetime experience, the story of which is new every day from that first moment onward. Just like the Eucharist!

These moments are a two step revelation for us. First of all, it remains clear that we are undeserving, unworthy of the gift, that we are sinners first and foremost. Everything tells us that somehow we should not have been invited to be one with Christ.

However, we also find ourselves forgiven. Thus we are invited. We are cleansed. We are healed. Also clearly this love of God lifts us up to begin to live life in a new way, in a way actually quite beyond ourselves. By virtue of the love that our Lord has for us, we find ourselves awakened to live somehow now in Christ. Our lives no longer need to be in our own possession. We can give them over to Our Father in heaven, and to the Christ walking with us.

All this, for Creatures of Dust!

While not perfect at this — we still have that sizable portion of that dust within us — we find ourselves drawn again and again, deeper and deeper into the love of Christ. In Christ, miracles happen on a daily basis. We hear his voice as we try to navigate this postmodern world. We find ourselves in dialogue with the Lord. We are now, for the first time, at home in this world, at home despite this Century being such a junkyard of meaning. In the midst of this, we are exactly at home in Christ!

We also now can understand the Mass and Eucharist that Christ has placed at the center of our faith. Week by week, and sometimes day by day, we approach the altar of the Eucharist, still keenly aware of our sinfulness, but overwhelmed that Christ would choose to come and dwell with us, to live within us.

Final Step of the Incarnation

Right there, we have the antidote to this age, the template of how to live in this era. The Eucharist is the final step of the incarnation, extending that entry into humanity, starting long ago with one young woman, Mary, destined to become the Mother of God. From her humble yes this sacred incarnation has come all the way to us at the present time.

There is an orientation that happens to us, that goes on especially within that Eucharist. Receiving Christ again and again reorients us to living in a new way in this world. This new ordering that flows from Christ's presence deep within us, strengthened by each reception of the Eucharist, leads us to reshape the dust that has been passed on to us from the days of Adam. We are led into the new beginnings of a redefined person, filled with the presence of Christ, anchored in eternal life, and oriented by the gifts of the Holy Spirit. Eventually Christ would have us be saturated in the flow of God's grace.

This reorientation of the Spirit and the presence of the Risen Christ with us is what gives us our primary tools to address and comprehend the empty, inverted universe of Satan. This presence gives us an understanding of these times, how they are wandering goofily about this 21st Century, as they attempt to reduce all truth and goodness into endless and meaningless variables.

16. Gracelessness

- What then? Shall we sin because we are
  not under the law but under grace? Of
  course not! Do you not know that if you
  present yourselves to someone as obedient
  slaves, you are slaves of the one you obey,
  either of sin, which leads to death, or of
  obedience, which leads to righteousness?
  But thanks be to God that, although you
  were once slaves of sin, you have become
  obedient from the heart to the pattern of
  teaching to which you were entrusted.
  Rom. 6:15-18

The Gift of Grace

Grace is the gateway to everything divine, everything transcendent. Grace is everything that lifts
us upward, beyond the limits of our human nature, and out of the mortality of our sinfulness.
Grace, the love of God, is the breathtaking rescue
from all that would destroy us, from all that
would mark our tombstones as the final end to
our existence.

This gift of grace is encapsulated in the dying and
rising of Christ our Savior, and showered upon us
by the Spirit. Grace appears in the Eucharist. We

stand in awe of what God Our Father has done for us in this gift.

How that grace changes us! How we are called to live in a way beyond our abilities, above our natural tendencies!

We are endlessly shocked and mystified that somehow God's love has become a part of who and what we are. We are constantly aware that in no way are we deserving, in no way have we earned what this gift is doing for us. Somehow, this gift of grace is always beyond us, yet always present to us. Grace is never in our control, yet always in our reach. It is remarkable how we are touched by this gift from above, so beyond us or so beyond our abilities and our limitations.

The Tragedy of Lost Grace

However, what happens, if through some strange upheaval, this gift of grace is absent? What happens, if in this postmodern era grace has been misplaced as it were, forgotten to the level of total amnesia? What happens without the least sliver of recall that there ever was something known as the love of God for us?

This is the tragedy of our times, this gift of grace, not just lost or misplaced, but rejected as pure fiction, or mere illusion. In the absence of belief in either a Father in heaven or his Son, the grace that flows endlessly and abundantly from above is as invisible as a rainbow at night, or the stars at noon.

In the presumed absence of grace, there are all kinds of consequences. Humanity is redefined. Morality becomes a fugitive. Hope dissipates. The most devastating piece in such a scenario is that humanity is left pursuing every possible avenue in a kind of endless string of horizontal behaviors. Humanity is left to try to lift itself to some sort of value and purpose in this world. For the human soul, gracelessness spirals away downwards full of frustration and fatigue. Such absence of grace never ever can find the meaning of the mystery of life. Such gracelessness is the tragedy of the secular era.

A Refusal of God's Grace

This postmodern era is in denial that there is anything such as the grace of God. Our era is incredulous that the grace from Christ our Savior is precisely the only thing on which to base our lives. The assumption is that grace is nonexistent, never was, or is even impossible to imagine. The world thinks there is no such thing as God's grace.

Even more, finding such grace to live by would require turning our hearts and minds both to Our Father in heaven and to the presence of the risen Christ in our midst. As a result, grace is not just something unable to be found, but rather something today often consciously refused! Thus, this is the era of chosen gracelessness.

Some would say that the heart of the matter is that we need to redefine our Christianity. In this grace-free climate, we should dumb down our faith, so to speak, to be something that humanity could achieve on its own. This era would have us assume that whatever our nature is, it is enough just by itself. There would appear no need of grace in such a scenario.

We can see the consequences of this choice — and it is a choice — whereby we are supposedly able to accomplish all things on our own. With nothing more than our human powers, human beings are supposedly to create our individual lives solely from whatever human power we might be able to conjure up on our own. This is the essence of gracelessness.

In essence, the assumption of this Century is that grace from above in impossible, is nonexistent, and is at best illusionary. This assumption is more than an ignorance of grace. I believe it is an active rejection, a bleak decision of the postmodern world.

This argument raises the sin against the Holy Spirit to a new level. There is no Holy Spirit in this realm of the secular! No wonder the sin against the Holy Spirit is unforgivable! There would be no one to whom to confess. There would be no one above to whom to turn.

What an incredibly bleak world!

The Consequence of Gracelessness

The central dividing line in all of existence is the line between grace and gracelessness. In grace we are oriented towards what comes to us from above, from Our Heavenly Father and his Son, the risen Christ, present in our times. In gracelessness, there is no one but ourselves alone.

We are right back to the moment of Adam and Eve's sin, where they make themselves like God. Gracelessness admits to none of the truth that we are beings who derive our lives from above. Without some sort of contact with faith and trust in the love of God, anyone would be left with the consequences of gracelessness.

The consequences of such a choice are legion! Here's some of those consequences.

The Primacy of Uproar

One of the first consequences of gracelessness is the constant uproar of our times. More than ever many seem to have this spirit of uproar, whether on facebook or twitter, about politics or on gender issues. There is no peace in gracelessness.

Human rights, multiply and evolve as never before, with new rights morphing and accelerating almost year by year. One is constantly surprised by what next new right within our culture has suddenly emerged, rubber stamped by the supreme court. All this is ungrounded, without an anchor, because of the absence of the divine in our culture.

What's worse, those who don't agree to the new rights are subjected to shaming and accused of bigotry. Hence divisions grow, dialogue dies in the face of this righteous uproar. For some reason, those who do hold to grace have become a threat to those who live in gracelessness, and have to be ostracized somehow.

There is a quote, supposedly from Nietzsche, that says if you unchain the earth from the sun, you end up with a world in total darkness. I suspect that when you disconnect the world from God above, you end up falling into this kind of uproar.

There Is No Forgiveness

Also noticeable in the realm of gracelessness is the absence of forgiveness. It appears that very little can ever be forgiven anymore. Everything is an opportunity for punishment, for bringing someone down, leading them to be ostracized, dismissed, fired, or subject to humiliation. There is no grace in gracelessness.

As a result, it appears that there is no such thing as healing. Once someone is shamed or humiliated for even the smallest of mistakes, there really is no road back anymore. They deserved it!

On top of that, no one can anticipate what the next frontier for shaming and punishment might be. That frontier is grounded nowhere, rooted in nothing, open daily to any new advance in righteousness. There is no moral reference point anymore, again, no anchor. Where God is absent, there is no center.

There are strict and hidden rules that, once violated, bring about a downfall. Anyone can declare themselves a victim today, and require the supposed perp to take a major hit, without protection or legal recourse. Micro becomes macro. This all brings scapegoating to a new height, all done by innuendo or inference. The proof is that my feelings have been hurt, thus the resulting in consequences without proportion. Everyone should now be the one able to cast the first stone!

Here's an idea: only sinners can truly forgive. More often than not, the accusers appear to live in a castle of perfection. In that castle, there is no sin, thus forgiveness is an alien in that place.

Forgiveness is an absolute fugitive in today's media and internet. Forgiveness would betray some major weakness. Forgiveness can't be a part of this climate of gracelessness.

How strange we who are disciples of Christ must seem today. Of course we are sinners, thus formed and shaped to forgive each other, just as our Father in heaven brought forgiveness to us. Schooled in the forgiveness that has come from above, we are living in a world that seems a new kind of wasteland.

The Ghost of Identity

Part of the tragedy of gracelessness is its impact on identity. Once the connection from above is gone, from the awareness of our creation by God, there is no way for the individual to take on an identity that has any substance. Thus, contemporary humanity struggles and wanders in search of an identity that should be here, but in fact, is not here.

By our very nature, humanity is one half of an equation, a being that cannot explain its existence in any fashion. Without our relationship to the divine, who are we? Who can we be in that context? The very nature of our being, or of our existence says that we are inexplicable by ourselves. We are a kind of reference point to something else. Without that something else, we remain undefinable.

For centuries on end humanity has understood that this connection came from above, even when it was locked in mystery. Humanity still knew they were from someplace else, and belonged to another realm somehow. This connection only reached completion in Jesus Christ, in his incarnation and his dying on the cross.

This coming of Christ completes our journey to know who we are and why we are here. The touchstone of this completion is our personal acceptance of Jesus Christ as our Redeemer, and in our openness to our Father in heaven. Once at this point, our identity not only falls into place, but lifts us into the realm of the sacred. That lifting up is the action of grace.

Gracelessness leaves identity as a human cipher. Gracelessness leaves us without definition. In gracelessness there is no one to lift us up. When we are not connected somehow beyond ourselves to Jesus Christ, identity is a ghost, something that should be, but just is not! For many, this is the tragedy of the 21st Century.

Desperation in Camouflage

One of the results of gracelessness is desperation. However, this form of desperation does not look like desperation. Rather, this gracelessness looks like liberation, total freedom, or self fulfillment. Thus, desperation appears wearing a costume that is the opposite of what it actually is. This desperation manifests itself as a kind of entitlement to do and become anything desired. On the surface it looks like the ultimate success, but is really much less so from within.

Desperation in this era of the secular amounts to an endless search for meaning, like scouring a junkyard for gold treasure. To compensate for this climate of desperation, life consists of a series of endless episodes, a search for prosperity and enjoyment that is never satiated. Gracelessness is the endless search for what can't be found.

A graceless world is a world that must try everything possible to find happiness, that we have to have whatever we want. The world without the presence of God's grace is most easily revealed in whatever new form of sexual experience our postmodern world now approves. A graceless world is lost in the absence of the value of marriage and family, in the scandal of abortion, in the sanctification of the profit motive to unheard of extremes.

On the surface gracelessness looks like self satisfied fulfillment, but underneath it hides an ocean of fragmentation and dissipation. This gracelessness is really the story of an era that has lost the major premise of existence, namely, the presence of Jesus Christ and the love of the Father in heaven. Without the connection to grace, there is nothing but a string of episodes, without beginning or end. Without the turn to Christ and faith, there is nothing but a horizontal, two-dimensional flatland, where successes only count when the next one is more than the last one. Needless to say, it cannot but end in an absence of peace and harmony. Life without Christ, existence without the Father from above has nowhere to go, no reason to carry on, no power to endure suffering. There is no love for the poor in such a two dimensional world. In short, without grace, there is no gateway to the transcendental. No wonder suicides keep increasing! No wonder that opioids are so beyond control! No wonder we witness the gun massacres that are so frequently in the news these days!

This secular era is a strange and twisted era. Absent the ability to lean on the presence of Christ or the gift of the Holy Spirit, there is little hope for reaching upward, or for allowing God's grace to reach downward into the depths of the soul. I truly think the first work of being Catholic today should start with prayer for humanity!

17. Singularity In Christ

- The fruit of the Spirit is love, joy, peace,
  patience, kindness, generosity, faithfulness,
  gentleness, self-control. Against such there
  is no law. Now those who belong to Christ
  Jesus have crucified their flesh with its
  passions and desires.
  Galatians 5:23-24

Our Deepest Identity: Purity and Chastity

The key to knowing most deeply who we are in
this world often has to do with our purity and
chastity. Purity and chastity are sacred states,
whatever our status in this world. This is a sacred
identity in marriage and family, in the celibate life
of the priesthood, in the choice of virginity, and in
the single state. Each state is unique, but somehow each is called to this one high form of life,
fully capable only in a life united with Christ.

Purity and chastity are not negative states.
Rather, they are the deepest possible identity that
we can have, whatever the state of our lives. We
cannot be more human than in purity and chastity, addressed both within ourselves, or between

ourselves. These states are not negative states, but are what is most sacred in the deepest part of our humanity.

One of the Keys to Salvation

Here in the 21st Century, there is no topic more relevant to the subject of purity and chastity than that of grace. Just to make it more interesting for us, there is probably no topic more conflicted or more violated today than that of purity and chastity. We should not shy away from putting this topic into a context of grace.

We have watched the boundaries to unbridled sexual expression fall over the past 60 years. Along with that massive change, we have seen crisis after crisis as our Catholic faith is repeatedly shaken by events, laws, and consequences driven by such unbridled behaviors. The breakdowns have occurred both within the culture, and within the Catholic world itself. From the 1960's onward, there is almost a continuing downward spiral of loss occurring decade by decade from the standpoint of Christian morality. All of this loss has been done in such a way as to suggest that this new sexual freedom is something to which we should have a right.

Morality has witnessed sexual permissions and abuses that are just stunning compared to previous times. Even within the Catholic community it-

self, we are stunned with shame and embarrass-
ment at what has happened.

On top of that, there is the apparent groundless-
ness of 21st Century morality, severed as it is from
its roots within Christianity, so that there is little
more than an aimless, incoherent and divisive
contest of wills and desires.

God's plan was never that we would reach purity
and chastity by ourselves, but would learn to lean
on the power of the presence of the risen Christ.
In Christ we are to come to lean on the gifts of
grace that the Holy Spirit would shower upon us.
In Christ all things are possible. Without Christ,
there is just this strange, inverted, alternative universe of Satan, where sexuality warps into a thousand different illusions about who and what we
could be.

This is the core of the issue before us, regarding
sexuality, purity and chastity. It is either the grace
of God with us, or a chaos of sexual behaviors.
Without the call of the Gospel, pointing us towards redemptive grace, our human identity
stumbles along without any intrinsic way to deal
with this sacred element of ourselves, much less
with the chaos of these postmodern times.

21st Century Capitulation

Part of our culture, now, is thrilled with what is
now permissible, but what was formerly prohibit-

ed. Another part is simply stunned by the immorality that is championed today. Seldom has there been a greater dividing point than what has defined sexuality, purity and chastity in the past two thousand years.

All of what has defined heterosexual and homosexual activities, the recognition of the addictions to pornography, everything relating to marriage and family, everything about the dignity of man and woman: all this is close to being shattered in this postmodern world of permissiveness.

On top of all that change, we as Catholic, struggle to understand what has gone wrong, or what we are to grasp in order to address the meaning of these changes that our culture seems so excited to embrace. On the one hand, we stand watching as the culture sinks into a kind of swamp of permissiveness. Sometimes, we find ourselves drawn into participation or approval of some sort.

On the other hand, we know deep in our hearts that such behavior is in absolute contradiction to all that we believe. Ultimately we can't square this permissiveness of the 21st Century with what the Scriptures so clearly speak, and what our faith has consistently taught us for two thousand years.

What went wrong?

At its core, humanity's struggle with sexuality comes close to the most fundamental weaknesses of our nature. From our catholic standpoint, our struggles with sexuality are right up there with all the other capital sins. Given the times, left to our own resources, we are about as weak as we can conceive regarding our human natures, fallen in the choice of Adam and Eve.

Instead of the honor and dignity afforded to all that is connected to the sacredness of the human body and soul, the contemporary world has decided that any and all sexual choices are available and open to any and all who would so choose. As a result there is this cascade of birth control, abortion, infidelity to marriage, the redefinition of marriage and all the gender dysphoria current today.

Perhaps, this freedom of choice is less than a choice than an acknowledgement. This acknowledgement exists because, without the grace from above, there is virtually no alternative to the kind of chaos today regarding our sexuality. Purity and chastity are hunted fugitives in this postmodern era.

It is as if this era is saying that, if we can't rise above our nature by ourselves, then we should just give in, and just consecrate the status quo, that anything goes. If there is no grace, if there is no doorway to grace, — and that is the assumption of these times — there is nothing left but such permissiveness and living within the lowest common denominator possible.

In addition, there is one area that this era has not been willing to examine at all. That area is the question of what happens to human dignity, what happens to the nature of man and woman in this free for all landslide into permissiveness. What happens to the dignity of children and youth? Where is humanity going in all of this?

When and if I can have anything I want, most likely I will get it by taking it away from another. Almost always, such choices seem to end in an exploitation. Almost always, that ends also in some often hidden form of destruction.

Further, we as Catholic have not definitively focused all our hearts and minds to live in exactly the way to which Saint Paul calls us. His Epistles call all to a purity and chastity that would rise above any and all the sexual permissiveness that he had so roundly condemned in the Roman world. This new Christianity had committed itself to live in this new Gospel manner, to overcome the inhumanity so prevalent at that time.

In all of this struggle, we need to know that it is the grace that flows from our baptisms and from the love of God alone that can teach us to live in this New Testament way. This is precisely the life style that we as Catholics are call to live. There is no question but that this New Testament life style is what we are called to as Catholic.

The Sacred Vessels

In the Mass, we cherish the vessels that are used to hold the Body and Blood of Christ, the chalice which holds the blood of Christ, and the ciborium which is used to hold the sacred Body of Christ. To us, the sacredness of these vessels is without parallel. All these vessels are lined with some form of gold leaf on the inside. Each instrument is artistically and beautifully constructed. Such vessels are set aside, locked up when not in use, kept perfectly clean, purified and dedicated for only the one use.

Our bodies are similar, precious in their intent and purposes, meant always for a divine purpose, vessels for the presence of Christ. First and foremost in our bodies is the gift of our sexuality, directed always to the possibility of bringing new life into our world. There is a purity about this, a clarity that is foundational to who and what we are. This focus is lodged deeply in the truth of our creation, and even clearer in the truth of our redemption.

Our flaw in this purity, of course, is our weakened natures, so easily out of focus, vulnerable to our selfish and possessive desires. Our hearts and souls still stand close to the addiction that comes from a lack of purity and chastity, with us stumbling again and again.

Satan's voice in all this is to remind us of our failures, an invitation to cease trying to live up to that which is so difficult in our hearts and minds. Quite frankly, left to ourselves, purity of the type to which the Scriptures call us is somewhat beyond what we in our weakened natures can possibly cope with by ourselves. Only in grace do we become what we ought to be. To be in the grace that comes from above has always been the only true and sure way of living the Gospel.

Satisfied in Our Fallen State

Our secular world says "Why fight it?" If we cannot be strong enough in ourselves to limit our choices sexually, in terms of purity and chastity, why not just say that all is allowed. After all, aren't we free to do as we want. That's what "choice" in the abortion world is all about. Pregnancy is just an obstacle to that freedom of choice, so birth control has to be an option. Choice in sexual matters fits nicely into the same realm as abortion. Supposedly, nothing could be more logical, given our human nature!

But what is missing here? Why not just "consecrate" all those sexual behaviors as acceptable now in this secular era. After all, purity and chastity are impossible now, more than ever. Isn't that why birth control is so important, why abortion is so necessary in this culture? The purpose of such logic is to allow us out to disregard the failures to live up to such an impossible ideal as purity and chastity.

The essence of the problem is that, of course, it is not possible without Christ that we could ever live with the kind of purity and chastity to which we are called. Of course not, not on our own! That was never the calling of the Lord to us, that we would live in such a way just on our own. The Gospel presupposes the gateway of grace. The Gospel says that all can be done in Christ.

The realm of the secular is a realm without the presence of the grace of God. The realm of the secular is quite simply that a life given to purity is simply an impossible myth of the fallen state of man, passed on from ancient times. In that realm, the sexual purity and chastity to which the Scriptures are calling us is simply impossible. In that context all is allowed, even exploitation for the sake of my needs. In that context exploitation is always just around the corner.

There is no grace in this secular outlook, just as there is no meaning to life in the secular era. The truth simply amounts to whatever your opinion is, to whatever you want. Human will is everything! Again, without Christ, you have this strange and inverted alternative universe of Satan, where sexuality warps into a thousand different illusions about who and what we are. No wonder there is so much sexual fatigue is this postmodern world. This is now often a world where sex is simply one episode after another, without any meaning or commitment, a free for all of personal exploitation.

The Consequences

In effect, given the secularism of our times, the logical conclusion would be that your sexual desires, whatever they might be, should be allowed and encouraged. The contemporary times say, "let's just consecrate the status quo, since we can't avoid it anyway."

These times say, "You should do anything you want, so long as it is private and self fulfilling. Since controlling those desires is at root impossible, the healthiest thing you can do is to entertain every option out there, and enjoy them."

The presumption is that there is no such thing as the grace of God that comes from above, no such thing as giving your life over to Jesus Christ. Sexuality then becomes a kind of string of episodes of whatever you might choose to experience. All this is allowable, of course, if there would be no such thing as grace from above. All this is allowable, since the assumption is that God is dead.

This makes marriage just one option, one no longer permanent. The commitment at the wedding would be just words. This makes children an obstacle of self fulfillment. Actually, this new state of sexuality empowers men especially to center themselves around sex, and consequently, makes woman especially an instrument of male self satisfaction. This also makes pregnancy a kind of health problem, requiring abortion at will!

This leaves religion, especially Catholicism, something to be seen as an enemy, one erroneously holding back the implementation of this new sexuality of the 21st Century. All of this, then, is arising from the newly defined and liberated sexuality of the postmodern world. It is a world devoid of transcendence and grace, absent God's love. This is another dimension of the emptiness of our times, of lives without Christ at the center. No wonder the hostility that Catholics face today!

The Resiliency of Confession

The living presence of Christ with us is what makes real the new state of grace, proclaimed by St. Paul so forcefully in the first days of the Church. Those first Christians were called to live in this new way in that pagan, chaotic time. That is what makes real the same possibility for the catholic of today. We have, in Christ, the way in which to live consecrated, holy lives, whatever our state, in the midst of this absurd, inverted alternative universe of Satan of the 21st Century.

In addition, as catholics, we have the added gift of the Sacrament of Confession, always available to us. Just because we have God's grace, we don't abrogate human nature, and the weaknesses that have come down to us from the time of Adam. We are still one foot in, and one foot out, when it comes to the kingdom of God.

In addition, this Sacrament received again and again in our lifetime brings a gift of grace that is unique to that Sacrament. This Sacrament involves a true healing from the inside out. In Confession Christ truly gives us a strength that rises above our human weaknesses. This sacrament of Confession teaches us to never give up!

This value of the Sacrament of Confession tips us off to the need for frequency and fidelity, without which our commitment to every aspect of our moral life is undermined. Confession, done frequently, schools us to never give up in our desire to live fully in Christ. Confession is one of the key antidotes to the permissiveness and immorality of this era, a true gift of Christ with us.

In essence, grace from above, flowing from the presence of Christ with us, is the secret of our catholic, human lives. In Christ, we never quit!

Grace redefines who and what we are, how we are to live, and what we are to become. Grace is the key to this secular age, the gateway to our new life, our entry to the new creation, of being lifted up to become what it was that was God's original intent in our creation.

Grace is not beyond us, once we begin to live in Christ Jesus, our Redeemer. Grace is not impossible for the average disciple of Christ. Grace is not for the elite. Grace belongs to all of us who try to follow the path of Jesus in our lives. Grace consecrates our purity and chastity. Grace lifts us above the evil of the capital sins in our lives, and the wreckage of this secular era. Grace is the sanctification of our desire for purity and chastity.

18. Solidarity in Faith

- May the eyes of your hearts be enlightened, that you may know what is the hope that belongs to his call, what are the riches of glory in his inheritance among the holy ones, and what is the surpassing greatness of his power for us who believe, in accord with the exercise of his great might, which he worked in Christ, raising him from the dead and seating him at his right hand in the heavens, far above every principality, authority, power, and dominion, and every name that is named not only in this age but also in the one to come. And he put all things beneath his feet and gave him as head over all things to the church, which is his body, the fullness of the one who fills all things in every way."
Ephesians 1:18-23

Additional Dimension to Purity and Chastity

There is one more dimension to the challenge of purity and chastity in our times, and to life in the Spirit that calls us to rise above the absence of morality in this era. That dimension is solidarity. The challenge of these times is that we need to have a solidarity in our faith, a kind of oneness, a sense of unity, a spirit of community. In short, we need a renewed sense of church.

Our oneness with Christ is the primary and vertical dimension of this solidarity. Our oneness with each other, in Christ, is the other part, the horizontal dimension of our solidarity. This spirit of total oneness, both vertically and horizontally, is an absolute necessity today in the era of the secular.

We have to have an unbreakable unity, a one unassailable solidarity for the days ahead. This is especially true in the area of sexuality, purity and chastity. However it is also true of every other dimension of morality in our days.

There can be no compromise, no accommodating of our life style to meet secularism halfway. There can be no room for a loose interpretation of these elements of our faith. Nothing short of solidarity will protect us in this realm of permissiveness and dissipation. Things fall apart in 21st Century individualism, in an arena of self satisfaction and self aggrandizement. Our solidarity with each other within our Catholic way of life will be the final part of our protection in this context.

There is no more room in this solidarity for the kind of grand exceptions that our culture wants us to allow, or in a kind of cowardly spirit of compromise. We simply can't pick and choose what pieces of morality we want, and those from which we excuse ourselves. We are called to be one in solidarity in faith. Our strength in part derives from one another.

Grace is Primary

There is this tendency among Catholics, historically, to look upon the commandments and the law as an obligation that falls primarily upon ourselves. Thus, it is an imperative upon us to fulfill those obligations. This stands out historically among Catholics. Such a tendency ignores our need to rely on our total love for Christ, and instead redirects the whole burden back upon ourselves.

All the weight is thus placed on our human nature. This, of course, is a blueprint for failure. We simply cannot succeed at these matters apart from Christ, apart from giving ourselves as fully to Christ as we can. This context of self reliance is one that Satan loves. In this context, Satan can always come back to remind us that we are failures. Satan is quick to tell us that we are incapable of living according to the call of the Lord. He is there to remind us that we simply can't do it. We, of course, then, end up in a kind of descending spiral where failure by ourselves leads to more failure.

Thus, we carry within our hearts a sense of failure, because we could not do it by ourselves. This tendency sets us up, as it looks to ourselves within our natures, to maintain all morality. Then, when we fail at doing it on our own, we end up in guilt and shame.

Satan absolutely loves that situation where we forget that it is only in Christ that we have any power, any forgiveness to start over, or any hope. This is Satan's best trap where one is imprisoned by desire, while forgetting the love of Christ. Satan constantly suggests that there is no way back.

The fact is, grace is not supplemental. Grace is primary in all our efforts. The power we have, even in our weakness, is the power to turn to Christ, to live within his mercy and love, and to never turn from what we know is his love for us. Christ can't help but share his grace and forgiveness with us when we are turned towards Him. He died on the cross to make that so. All we need do is to turn to Him.

The Source of Grace

Of course our effort and sacrifice is always necessary. In actual fact, the primary obligation, our primary effort is that we really have to give ourselves fully to Christ, sacramentally, especially in the Eucharist and in prayer. Only this way can we free ourselves of our own egos and selfishness, and the guilt and shame inherent within our old life style.

Living more fully in Christ is the first obligation we have. Then, Christ's presence with us will bring us to the level of grace so necessary in these secular times. External self control will never ever be enough for faith or morality today. Living more fully in Christ is the only step that will fully succeed, because Christ is alive and present to us, walking in our midst. He is clearly one with us whenever we turn to Him with all our hearts. In fact, there is nothing else!

In addition, Christ is not distant. He is not indifferent. He is not busy with other things. We are his project, the ones for whom he died on the cross. Christ is as close to us as if we could feel his heart beating. We are to be as close to Him as was Thomas at the moment Christ called upon him to place his hand in his side. Christ is that personal with us. If we allow Him that position in our lives, and stand in solidarity with each other, we will be that light shining in the darkness. In solidarity we will be precisely what Saint Paul described in his letter to the Philippians 2:15,

"That you may be blameless and innocent, children of God without blemish in the midst of a crooked and perverse generation, among whom you shine like lights in the world."

Grace is Primary, Held In Solidarity

Again, grace is not supplemental, but primary in all our spiritual life. That is grace, not willpower! It is grace, not by myself alone, but in union with Christ, and in solidarity with all who are disciples of Christ. Always, he is the fire at the center of the burning bush, as Moses experienced. Christ is always at the center, with all of us gathered in solidarity around Him.

The basis of our solidarity is exactly in Christ, in coming to live within the realm of grace, reaching as high and as deep as possible into the way highlighted and outlined within the New Testament. The call we have remains consistent from the 1st Century to the 21st. That is also a dimension of our solidarity.

Therein lies a deep part of our challenge, a kind of solidarity in grace with each other today, side to side, as well as with all those who have gone before us and those to come after us, start to finish. Also, we cannot live in community apart from the Eucharist, apart from Confession, apart from daily prayer and adoration. These are not ordinary times!

The Final Piece, Solidarity

While this may seem daunting, no one has ever successfully taught that such solidarity was possible except in the giving of oneself to Christ. The engine of our salvation is always to trust completely in God's grace and love. The final piece of our union with Christ is our oneness in faith, and our loving support of one another within the realm of the church. The final piece of our sanctity in these times is the solidarity we have as Christ's disciples. The first piece is singularity, the last is solidarity.

In the end, grace rules, if we give Christ our full attention. Once grace rules, we will have the kind of hope and peace to pour out on those of the 21st Century that are seeking to find the Savior of the world, but do not yet know Him.

There is a passage in the Gospel according to John, (Ch 14) that reads as follows: Jesus said:

- "The Advocate, the holy Spirit that the Father will send in my name — he will teach you everything and remind you of all that I told you."

This means, I think, that the Holy Spirit will keep us in understanding with what Christ has taught in the beginning, as well as to apply that teaching crossways to our times. The Advocate reaches into the present, keeping us in line with with the Word that has been revealed in Scripture in the beginning. Again, it is singularity coupled with solidarity.

Taught by Christ, kept in line by the Spirit seems to me to be the basis of our solidarity. What we teach and follow today must simply be in line with what was there in the beginning. This context brings us back to the rest of what St. Paul was teaching in Galatians, the rest of which this chapter began.

- In contrast, the fruit of the Spirit is love, joy, peace, patience, kindness, generosity, faithfulness, gentleness, self-control. Against such there is no law. Now those who belong to Christ Jesus have crucified their flesh with its passions and desires. If we live in the Spirit, let us also follow the Spirit.
Galatians 5:23-25

19. The Provocateur

- In the evening you say, 'Tomorrow will be fair, for the sky is red'; and, in the morning, 'Today will be stormy, for the sky is red and threatening.' You know how to judge the appearance of the sky, but you cannot judge the signs of the times. An evil and unfaithful generation seeks a sign, but no sign will be given it except the sign of Jonah.
Matthew 16:2-4

Our Strange Position in the 21st Century

The more we exist in this era, the more we can see that our situation as Catholics is perceived as awkward. All the values we carry forward from the Gospel, and all the ways of living that we hold deep in our hearts all seem somehow out of place as this Century unfolds. The hostility is palpable!

The list of disagreements that we face is endless: what marriage is, the centrality of family, purity and chastity, finding Christ within the poor, the sacredness of the unborn and children, the power of suffering and sacrifice. This Century continues to chip away at all of these treasures of morality and humanity. There we are, seeking to hold on to such treasures while living in an era such as this.

At the same time, our situation as Catholics is breathtaking, grounded in a reality that lifts us upwards into a realm of grace. This reality of grace rises above anything we deserve, or anything we could have anticipated or imagined. The call to live within God's love is awesome.

We need to have a feel for the gift of grace, and for what that gift does to us day by day. We need to sense the depth of the Mass and Eucharist. We need to reflect upon the dimensions of grace in our faith life, the forgiveness that has been extended to us.

There is a hidden dimension to what grace is doing to us. Christ in our hearts is as deep as the ocean, an ever flowing river of which we become a part. Never has our difference from these times been clearer. It is as far apart as awkward is from awesome.

The Ascendency of Faith over the Secular

I would like to suggest a scenario. This scenario is an alternative way of looking at what is happening in this 21st Century. It is a way of reinterpreting what this postmodern time is really all about.

The usual perspective suggests that Christianity is gradually being wiped out by the materialism and secularism of these times. It appears on the surface, that generation by generation, any semblance of Christianity is being massively atrophied and shrunken to virtually nothing.

This is especially true of our Catholicism, that particular way of Christianity, so supposedly divorced and irrelevant to the 21st Century. Our Catholicism is deemed the most inappropriate and obtuse of these postmodern times, destined for becoming some sort of obsolete remnant of the supposedly fictional and superstitious times of the past.

So far as these times are concerned, it's all over for us. We catholics didn't bend enough, and we were too stuck in dogma, history or teaching to have anything to say anymore in these times. We have been redefined as bigots, not promoters of the "new human rights" that bestows equality upon any and every human redefinition that people can think of. We are thought to be destined for nonexistence!

The Thing Which Cannot be Looked At

However, there is another perspective, another scenario to consider. In the above paragraphs, notice that there is one factor that seems to have been ignored or forgotten. The radical redefinition of humanity, so pursued in this 21st Century, seems to have intentionally forgotten one thing to mention: Jesus Christ, from whom and through whom all grace rains down into our lives. Oops!

This is a lacuna that is immense. This amnesia about Jesus Christ is too intentional to have been simply overlooked. It is one thing to have ignored the church, to have condemned Catholicism for being out of touch for these times. It is quite another, that Jesus Christ would somehow be missed!

In all honesty, it is not an oversight on the part of the postmodern world! Instead it is intentional!

This awareness about Jesus Christ is "the thing which cannot be looked at." The absence or presence of Christ today is the central foundational issue before all of humanity today.

There is good reason for this gap in the postModern awareness. Christ is simply too dangerous to know. Deep down, at the level of their bone marrow, Jesus Christ is the central question of our times, or of the secular world. His presence is looming over everything happening in this century.

Thus, the presence of Jesus Christ must be suppressed by this era. It cannot be approached. The presence of the risen Christ in our midst cannot have a place in the new identity politics and redefined human rights that appears to be the lifeblood of the postmodern, secular doctrines of the 21st Century. Ultimately, nothing could be more terrifying to this secular era than the mo-

ment of the coming of Jesus Christ, judge of the
world.

The One Who Is Coming

When I read and think about this 21st Century
and all its secular makeup, there appear to be two
separate explanations. The most popular one, is
that Catholicism has now been bested, lacerated
by the power of the secular. Sometimes, watching
the events and newly invented human rights that
surround them, Catholics can't help but start to
believe that there may be substance to what is
happening. The secular may win out!

However, there is another perspective, one on
which Catholics need to focus today. This perspective is that the incarnation of the Son of God,
coupled with his dying and rising, is the ultimate
provocative action on the part of God.

In essence, the Good News of the Gospel is a shot
across the bow of the world, requiring the whole
of the world to choose the redemptive grace of Jesus Christ, completely and totally. Based on this
divine intervention into the history of humanity,
soon no longer will the world be able to avoid the
fundamental decision regarding discipleship of
Jesus Christ.

In other words, the agent at work today, in this
21st Century, is not Satan, the forces of evil, or
the secularism that surrounds us. Those are in a

sense irrelevant to the issue at hand. The agent most at work is the Lord of all life, the Savior of the world, the Judge sitting at the right hand of the Father.

The Lord Jesus Christ, is provocatively forcing the modern world to confront this most fundamental question, a yes or no about the centrality of Christ. The agent at work in our times, Christ, is forcing from hiding the fundamental rejection of all that is transcendental. The presence of the risen Christ with us brings a critical choice to the surface, one no longer able to be hidden. The choice is either yes or no to Christ himself!

This source of the action puts what is happening in a totally different perspective. Instead of our Catholicism being overcome by the secularism of the 21st Century, we are witnessing the approaching triumph of the cross of Jesus Christ.

This era is being forced to acknowledge that Christ will not accept denial, but requires the humble, sincere repentance of all humanity. He will provocatively force the issue of secularism to run deeper and deeper until it destroys itself in its denial of the Savior of the world. On the other hand, this era has the option of finally acknowledging that Jesus Christ is in fact the Redeemer of the world. Christ's presence is clearly a constant provocation, requiring the world to choose.

In the end, the ultimate consequence of the incarnation of Jesus Christ into our world is that those who would ignore the coming of Jesus Christ will be left with only one other option. That option is a descent into a nothingness and a meaninglessness end of the secular.

Forcing a Decision

In other words, Jesus Christ is forcing the times to make the most fundamental decision possible: to choose him or to reject him. This is not the evolution of the secular, gradually grabbing space and time to master things. Instead, the world has been set up, brought to a final point of decision regarding Jesus Christ.

In sadness we have to say that the 21st Century is failing to choose discipleship with Christ. These times have pointedly turned its back on Him to go its own way in creation.

As we look at where we as Catholic have come from, and where this world in now going, the collision course was not set by those who have mastered the secular era, but by Christ's very coming into this world. At the time, the birth of Jesus seemed an innocent beginning of something new. That moment of incarnation was never imagined to be an act that would stop the world in its tracks. Not until now!

The 21st Century has revolted against this act so deeply and so egregiously, that we cannot help but think that this choice will ultimately and quickly bring about the end that the Scriptures have long predicted. His dying on the cross charted the decision point of all of history. There has always been an expectation that judgment is coming quickly. Perhaps we can now see that it is drawing very close.

However, the question, the dilemma that the postmodern world now has seems to warrant special concern about the end of things. Accept or reject the Lord Jesus Christ! Accept or reject the freedom that alone comes only from above! Accept or reject the kind of love that we have been called by Christ! It's down to a "yes" or a "no!"

Be clear, this dilemma is not stemming from the challenge of the secular era. The challenge is primarily the provocation by the incarnation of Christ in the world, his action on the cross, and his hidden, risen presence with true believers today. The Eucharist especially points to this moment and marks its proximity. There is no way out of this moment except to choose or to deny. No Excuses!

Satan's Inevitable Defeat

We who are living the life of faith have not lost our way, not fallen into irrelevancy in this 21st Century. Quite the opposite! Jesus Christ, risen and present within us, amounts to the final stumbling block, an immovable object to this era.

Christ will finally provoke the illumination and uncovering of a world that is soundly and irrevocably rejecting Him as Lord of this world.

However, to make the other choice, a humble, simple "Yes" to Christ, will still appear in time to bring about healing. In the end there will be no pretense of non-existence of God or Christ, no camouflaged disposition that humanity itself is god. There will be only the question of whether or not Jesus Christ is Lord of all.

Of course, Christ came to save all who would open their hearts to Him. Of course, He is the Savior of the world. But for centuries, Satan's inverted alternative universe has stalled the inevitable moment when the final choice must be made.

Ways to Accept Christ

I would be remiss had I not tried to illustrate that there are many ways to recognize the presence of Christ. When the individual turns toward the poor, reaches out to those in need, feeds the hungry — all of these and many others can be a form of saying yes to Christ. The saying of yes to Christ often begins with marriage and family. The way of the Spirit reaches far beyond the obvious, and seeks out many whose hearts are pure and open to brothers and sisters in need. The gateway of grace is not narrow or limited in any way. This gateway either explicitly or implicitly centers on Christ.

Satan and his minions of this 21st Century probably think that they are winning by spreading the message of denial and agnosticism. However, even that strategy provokes and ultimately hastens the final question, the final decision of every single human being. The further away this world goes from the Son and His Father, the closer the final decision comes. The question is, are we there yet? We surely draw close.

There are few things that are inevitable in this world. Some would say, death and taxes. However, on the stage of the world, only one thing is inevitable. It will be the moment when the world is forced to choose regarding Jesus Christ and his Father in Heaven. This decision will be up front, no more hiding, no more invisibility, no more dissembling.

The entire history of Christianity, the whole of the incarnation, and the truth of the cross is pointed to this moment. The more this world retreats into itself, the closer that moment comes. The more this world enters into secularism, the sooner the actual point of choice will become visible. It will be Christ or else. In the end there is nothing else, other than the nothingness of hell.

At the other extreme exists the beauty and the awesome gift of grace to anyone who would turn somehow to the Savior of the world. The grace of

God, the love of God surrounds anyone who in humility and spiritual poverty would turn to Christ in some fashion. This choice remains open to all, and will not fail anyone who so chooses.

20. The Cross, Identity and Grace

-   Thus not even the first covenant was inau-
    gurated without blood. When every com-
    mandment had been proclaimed by Moses
    to all the people according to the law, he
    took the blood of calves and goats, togeth-
    er with water and crimson wool and hys-
    sop, and sprinkled both the book itself and
    all the people, saying, "This is 'the blood of
    the covenant which God has enjoined
    upon you.'" In the same way, he sprinkled
    also the tabernacle and all the vessels of
    worship with blood.
    According to the law almost everything is
    purified by blood, and without the shed-
    ding of blood there is no forgiveness.
    Hebrews 9:18-22

What Is Intrinsic to Our Faith

The cross is intrinsic to the Catholic seeking to
live their faith fully in the 21st Century. Throughout history, those who seek to live their faith have
always known that the cross is essential to any
person of faith. That truth is especially so in this

21st Century. The cross is the contradiction to the postmodern world of entitlement.

This cross in this Century has many dimensions. However, whatever dimension, that cross has to include giving ourselves for another, and another, and yet another. This is the point where we separate ourselves from those of entitlement. It is not in getting, it is in giving, pouring ourselves out for others. In the cross we offer ourselves for the Gospel, and to Christ himself, ever present to us in this strangest of ages. The cross is the pouring out of self, again and again, without drawing the line, without a hiatus, without hesitation. All this, then, is done in our weakness fortified by grace. We are to seek the cross, clothed in all our frailty.

The Cross Misperceived

The cross often is perceived only as the one on which Christ hung until he died. The cross of Christ appears in most of our minds, to be a kind of total martyrdom, whereby you lose everything in excruciating pain. The cross of Jesus is what we are thinking about when we pray the last line of the Our Father: "Deliver us from evil." We pray that the Father would keep us safe from the kind of cross that Jesus had to endure, on his own, totally abandoned over to the power of evil.

This thought of the cross holds us back. We are afraid of the major, and thus avoid the lessor parts of the cross. At times in history that sacrifice somewhat like Christ's has been required, always in a context of great grace, with the abiding presence of Christ.

However, for most of the time, and for most of us, the cross shows itself in small ways, in the extra effort on our part to reach out to others, to go the extra mile in our family or neighborhood, to forgive even when we can't forget. Most of the time, the cross is what we do when we continue to serve, even when we are exhausted, or when we simply choose not to give up.

The cross is when we live for those around us, when we hear Christ calling us to do something new, to try to carry a little extra in our burdens in life. The cross is actually not something foreign or extreme beyond us. The cross is usually just the common everyday life, lived out as best we can, abandoning our selfishness.

The cross is even when it takes all your energy to just get out of bed in the morning. The cross is when you try to forgive a hurt. The cross is when you pray for those who have hurt you. The cross is for when you go on loving someone even when you don't like them at the moment.

The cross is a lot of little things. The cross is attentiveness. The cross is going the extra mile with someone. We are at our best when we do such things, when we find the cross that is within us today, and still do our best.

The Cross Already Present

We don't have to go looking for the cross. It exists already in our lives. Accepting the cross is mostly just acknowledging what is already there, or by what we are already burdened. We are often so afraid of the cross that might come, we suppress the cross we already have. Thus, instead of giving our energy and commitment to what is already there, we find ways to try to escape what it is within our lives that could redefine us in Christ. The cross is often synonymous with grace.

Often, because we are held back by either our fear of the future or by our resistance to the cross already in us, we miss something important. The acceptance of the cross is the power to live in a new way. The cross, lived out in grace, changes our identity, delivers a new depth to our personality, and redefines our purpose in this world.

The cross is the gateway to things that are transcendental, theological about our lives and our souls. Our individual cross opens us to the presence of Christ in a new way, taking us the rest of the way into the kingdom of God.

The acceptance of the cross erases our self-centeredness, gives us the gift of humility. The cross allows us to hear Christ himself speaking to us. The cross is a passageway, leading us deeper and deeper into what God's plan for us is and has been

from the moment of our conception. The cross is a
river of grace waiting to be poured out within us.

The Gift of the Cross

One of my classmates in the seminary, long ago,
received a letter from an oil company inviting him
to quit the seminary and join that corporation. In
the kicker at the end of the letter, the recruiter
wrote in an effort to entice him to join the man-
agement of that oil company:

"Upon the plains of hesitation,
rot the bones of countless millions,
who tiring, sat down to rest,
and resting died."

Needless to say, that seminarian went on to serve
the church as a priest for many years, never tiring
of serving the call that he had. He chose the cross,
without hesitation.

Probably the greatest enemy of the cross is just
giving up. The recruiter got it exactly backwards.
Choosing to take, rather than to give, is the heart
of both tiring and dying.

The Cross and Identity

This 21st Century seems to be preoccupied with
identity, every person seeking to define them-

selves in some unique fashion. Most often identity fails because identity cannot be achieved without oneness with Christ. We are not who we are until we reach that point of knowing Jesus Christ in our hearts, and of turning this life over to Christ.

In addition, the secret passageway to Christ is through the cross. In fact, there is no other passageway. The cross is it, different for each of us, but the real gateway to Christ and the new creation we are to be. The cross opens the cornucopia of grace to us.

The cross in our lives is not something in our future that we are invited into. Instead, the cross is today, in our life as it exists now. Nor do we have to go looking for the cross. We don't need to find some external cross, one we have to invent. We need not do self-flagellation. If we are looking for something really big as our cross, we are probably looking in the wrong place. The cross is not something we have to concoct. The cross is an intrinsic piece to who we are, and how we are to live. The cross is intrinsic to who we are.

We don't have to go looking for trouble. The cross is there every day. Sometimes in our life, "Armageddon" comes to us, some super critical cross that we just have to bear. These are rare, and are accompanied with a superabundance of grace and love on the part of Christ.

However, living the cross day by day, we are schooled by the Lord about the presence and gifts of God's grace and love. We are often awakened by whatever it is that cripples and handicaps us in small ways, The Spirit disarms the greater crosses in our lives to something that we can understand when it happens, and sends gifts to us that yield endurance for us in the face of anything.

The Realm of Grace in Our Identity

What the presence of Christ does for us is to teach us to fear nothing that this world can send against us. The inverted alternative universe of Satan of today is a creaky, collapsing junkyard attempt at duplicating what only the power of Christ can bring to us.

Ours is the realm of grace and divine love, of ultimate forgiveness, and of a lifting up of each of us into the realm of faith and hope. This is exactly what we find in the cross of Jesus Christ in our hearts.

In truth, the invitation to the cross is for today, how we are to give ourselves in these very real moments of our current life. The presence of Christ in our lives is what enlightens us to who we are, and to what we want to become. The cross opens the pathway to this total union with Christ, where we reach the point of being in Christ.

The one who wants to be a disciple of Christ doesn't find Christ by looking for Him. Instead one must find his or her cross, and that will reveal the living, risen Christ who walks near us, seeking to touch our souls, wanting to bring us to union with Himself.

Marriage and parenting work best when combined with the cross that reveals the presence of Jesus Christ in the home. That presence shines in our souls through the cross experienced in our daily life, in our home, in our giving of ourselves for one another. Only then do we take on an indelible identity, one not fashioned by whim or self-centeredness, one not defined by clothing or possessions, one not of bumper stickers or the national football league. This indelible identity from above is one not of guns, fishing rods or golf clubs, one not defined by alcohol or compulsion.

Identity in Christ

This indelible identity, that comes only from above, is most concrete when we give ourselves in the cross. This indelible identity is the only identity that will satisfy the deepest part of our soul. This indelible identity shines most when it has found the risen Christ, revealed in depth through the cross in our lives.

Clearly, the secret to this indelible identity is the cross. We must take the issue of identity one step further. Before we can experience the full scope of our identity, we must take it to the point of the cross. This identity only comes from above.

The roots of this identity were planted deep within us at the moment of our conception, possibly even from all eternity in the mind of God.

Somehow that identity must include the cross, this giving up of self, of yielding to the needs of the family and the community, of reaching out to the poor or to the less fortunate. But always, this cross starts at home, where we are living, what we do in the day. Only in the cross will the gift of grace disclose itself in us.

In short, we are to know who we are fully by accepting the cross where we experience Jesus Christ Himself, hidden in our very hearts. This step of the cross is the very heart of loving Christ. This step is the capstone of an indelible identity. Anything else leaves us with an emptiness and a dissatisfaction with what and who we are. An attempt at identity without the cross leaves us on an addictive journey towards sexuality and material satisfaction, stuck at the level of acquiring, but never possessing.

The Contradiction

What a hard step identity is when attempted without Christ or the cross. If it is "me" that is at the center of things, identity transforms into compulsion, pridefulness, or competition. Ultimately, if it is "me" at the center, there is an entitlement fatigue characteristic of the inverted alternative universe of Satan.

What then is lost is the deep possibility of an identity that the Father and the Son have placed within our mortal souls, one that is to last forever, one that alone is able to bring a spirit of true joy and tranquility to our hearts. How sad this postmodern world becomes. What could have been is not even imagined for many in these times.

The contradiction between entitlement and the cross is hard to exaggerate. Entitlement is a kind of addiction leading nowhere. In entitlement, the self becomes the form of divinity itself. Whenever we start from ourselves, the true divinity from above is blocked from our lives, leaving us fumbling around to find something that appears not to exist. Sadly, few will find the identity that God alone had in mind for them if they refuse the cross in order to pursue the mythical goblins of entitlement.

The Gift of Grace from Above

Last of all, we need to know that the cross comes with a comparable gift of grace from above. When we finally have the courage and determination to accept the cross an immense gateway of grace appears. This gift of grace from the cross showers us with both energy and trust, giving us an ultimate identity in Christ.

This grace brings with it courage and insight as to how to live. This grace brings with it a kind of knowledge and understanding unavailable to human wisdom. This grace brings with it ways to comprehend our sinfulness, our weakness, and all those tendencies that cripple us. This grace leads us to an awareness of Christ's absolute love for us that lifts us above our past.

The cross, then, is full of surprises, blessings, revelations, and wonderments that we could never ever have imagined. The cross is the touchstone of grace, not just to Christ Himself, but also to the eternal life where Christ would lead us and to the new creation that is far beyond anything we can imagine.

21. A Parable of Pegs and Pitch

- I kneel before the Father, from whom every family in heaven and on earth is named, that he may grant you in accord with the riches of his glory to be strengthened with power through his Spirit in the inner self, and that Christ may dwell in your hearts through faith; that you, rooted and grounded in love, may have strength to comprehend with all the holy ones what is the breadth and length and height and depth, and to know the love of Christ that surpasses knowledge, so that you may be filled with all the fullness of God.
Ephesians 3:14–19

A Little Investigation

I had known from childhood that my heritage was both German and Irish. About two decades ago, however, I was told that the Irish side had some Spanish blood in it. This was a surprise to me. Then I began a little investigation.

The roots of the Spanish seemed to come from a distant ancestor whose last name was Delmore. I

did not think that was a very Irish name, and began to suspect that it may have come from the
Spanish, something like "de la mar," from the sea.

The Spanish Armada

Then by chance I came across a study of the
Spanish Armada, written from the English view-
point. That study suggested that the armada consisted of mainly Spanish galleons, designed as
boarding ships for use in the South Atlantic.
These ships carried soldiers to board their oppo-
nents ships, using grappling hooks to swing
aboard the enemy vessel.

On the other hand, the British ships were "Men of
War," designed for speed and bombardment in the
North Atlantic. Sir Francis Drake's fleet was
sleek and speedy in that encounter with the
Spaniards.

The British were all sailors, rather than boarding
parties. The British thus avoided the galleons'
grappling hooks and simply pummeled them in
bombardment for hours, circling just out of range
with a speed the galleons couldn't match, completely outmaneuvering the awkward Spanish
ships not designed for this kind of naval battles.

The defeated Spanish ships fled, some grounded
on the shores of Northern Europe, and a few oth-

ers attempted to circle north to go around Scotland and Ireland, and then south to Spain.

These escaping ships that circled north suffered greatly from the North Atlantic. Their ships were constructed with the use of pegs and pitch, sufficient for the South, but not for the coast of Ireland or the storms and waves of the North Atlantic. Numbers of them simply fell apart from the pitch and yaw of the wind and waves of the North Atlantic, washing them up as a kind of rubble on the beaches and rocks of the West of Ireland.

You could visualize the ships, with the pegs that held the frame together gradually loosening, the pitch used to fill the cracks coming undone and pulled apart.

Those ships that had escaped around the north were in danger of becoming nothing but drifting piles of boards after weeks in the North Atlantic. The drainage pumps were unable to keep up with the leakage. The flotsam and jetsam, with a number of survivors, in the end, washed up on the rocky coast of Ireland.

My belief is that a few of the Spaniards must have survived that dreadful experience, as well as some from the efforts of the British to exterminate the Spanish survivors. One of those would have to been a branch of my ancestors.

The likelihood of this story, I think, stems from the secrecy and hiddenness that the elderly of my

Irish relatives carried for many years about one part of their heritage.

An Image for the 21st Century

I share this story, only from the image of the ships constructed with pegs and pitch, clearly inadequate for the place where they were attempting to sail. It's that painful breakup that interests me.

The real issue here in the 21st Century is an environment where all connection with the transcendental, theological realm of life is simply absent. There is no longer any "above" from which anything of value comes. The result is a time where all thing tend to break apart. We are watching the breakup of the pegs and pitch of the 21st Century, a collapse where everything is slowly coming apart, given the environment of these times. What follows are a few examples of that collapse.

Meaning Today

First there is meaning itself. Given the absence of the divine in peoples' lives, much of the meaning in life has fallen apart. Meaning's now a junkyard of broken pieces, equivalent to the debris of the Spanish armada that lost its pegs and pitch in the constant wave action of the North Atlantic.

Without meaning, truth becomes a fugitive. Without meaning, common sense is gone. Without meaning, shouting replaces dialogue. This is because meaning only comes from above. Meaning cannot be constructed from within ourselves, but is derived from knowing from where we have come, why we are here, and what our purpose of existence is. Ultimately, the full extent of meaning in this world derives from the love of God, the presence of Christ and the Spirit hovering over us, showing us how everything fits together.

Hope Today

Then, there is the matter of hope. With the amnesia of the culture today regarding Christ and the Father in heaven, all that is left are only mere fragments of horizontal hope. Without a knowledge of the love of God for us, hope amounts to picking ourselves up by the bootstraps.

True hope only comes from above. It is theological. No one is capable of deriving hope at the animal, horizontal level of life. Where there is nothing divine or theological, nothing transcendental in peoples lives, there is only a kind of wilderness devoid of hope. Only leftover fragments remain in a two dimensional wasteland. What remains in secularism is like the fragments of the armada, washed up on the beaches and rocks of Ireland.

Without a theological sense of hope, we are like those on board the ships of the armada, watching the pegs and pitch gradually being wiggled loose, and the timbers of the ships weakening to the point of crumbling into a pile of boards to be washed nearer and nearer to the rocky coast of Ireland.

Frankly, there is nothing from this world that that can give hope. We live on a planet evolving at its own independent pace, going wherever it wants. In our human sinfulness, we continue to create more negative climate change, more and more weapons of destruction, with an ever increasing avarice. Hope will have to come from elsewhere!

Morality Today

Then, there is morality in this era, looking very much like the ships of the armada that couldn't handle the pitch and yaw of the North Atlantic. All that is left of morality is this flotsam and jetsam of the collapse, connected to nothing. The only connection for morality has to come from above. Today, outside of faith in Jesus Christ, there is no "above" to which morality could be connected. Thus all morality is in chaos. Thus, there exists this moral shipwreck of this 21st Century.

As a result, the existence of any stable morality has come unhinged from what is above. Our morality must of necessity come from what is theological and transcendent. True morality must be built on a foundation that is divine.

Morality is simply impossible in these times apart from a theology! As a result, morality has eroded to the point of nothingness in the secularism of our times. Whatever pegs and pitch that held it together before are now loosened and lost, drifting like collapsing ships from the armada, waiting for the final breakup.

The Challenge to Catholicism

We as Catholic today find ourselves in an environment that is toxic to the faith, in this era of the secular. We need to know that we are living in an environment of sexual permissiveness and unrestrained greed.

The pegs and pitch that we have used to maintain our faith from the past are simply insufficient for the pitch and yaw of the postmodern world. Often we, as Catholics, have coasted along with a minimal effort, without grasping deeply the roots of our faith in this secular time. Nor have we noticed the dangers!

If we are in trouble faith-wise in these times, there are two causes. Most likely first it is because we have been inattentive to what has been happening over the course of these fifty to seventy year in American life.

Secondly, in addition to underestimating the secularism of our times, we have not yet grabbed onto what it is that is of the essence of living out our Catholicism. We cannot exist in this era without the presence of Christ walking with us. We must have the centrality of the mystery of the Eucharist, and the foundational support of the Sacrament of Confession. We need nothing short of a daily, personal sense of prayer. These things are of the essence of who and what we have to be as Catholics today.

We had thought that Sunday morning was sufficient to sustain us in our Catholicism. We may have often drifted for six days out of the week in this soup of secularism. We may have assumed that this climate is merely neutral to faith. However, in reality this era is toxic to anything spiritual. This era is becoming the antithesis of what Catholicism has to be. No wonder, there is such antagonism against everything Catholic today.

Nothing short of a deeply held, strongly professed commitment to Christ will be sufficient. The Holy Spirit is propelling us to live much more deeply in our faith than ever before. That Spirit is calling us to anchor ourselves fully in the mysteries that the Mass centers on, to rivet ourselves totally to the risen Christ in whom alone we can sail this sea of secularism.

An awareness of the gift of grace from above would go a long way towards helping us discern the difference between our Catholic faith and the secular world in which we are living. The safety of our religious lives gets no help from a secular culture, only a kind of invisible undermining, similar to the pitch and yaw of galleons adrift in the North Atlantic.

As catholics, we have at hand an invincible resource of support in the cross of Christ, in the gift of grace, and in the absolute love of the Father for us. All of these gifts are summarized and united in the Sacrifice of the Mass. These gifts are precisely the resources we need as Catholics to address these times!

22. Abandonment

-   From noon onward, darkness came over
    the whole land until three in the afternoon.
    And about three o'clock Jesus cried out in
    a loud voice, "Eli, Eli, lema sabachthani?"
    which means, "My God, my God, why
    have you forsaken me?"
    (Matthew 27.26-27)

Disturbing Words

To us who are "non-exegetical," and not very theological, there are probably few more disturbing
words of Jesus than these words that Jesus spoke
on the cross: "My God, my God, why have you
forsaken me?"

Did Jesus give up? Did the Father really abandon him, forsake him totally? Did Jesus fail his
Father? What was going on here? Why wouldn't
his Father stay with him, instead choosing other-
wise, choosing to abandon his Son. Right at the
moment of deepest need on the part of the dying
Jesus, the Father left Him alone in a storm of total hopelessness? After all, it was the Father that
put Him up to this task. The first time I heard
these words of Jesus on the cross, I found them
disturbing.

Only later did I realize that Jesus was quoting a particular psalm, Psalm 22. When I looked more closely at that psalm, I realize that actually it is a psalm of absolute faith and trust in the power of the Father, resulting in a prayer of total praise, even in the midst of adversity. It reads in part, verses 24-27:

- All descendants of Jacob, give honor;
  show reverence, all descendants of Israel!
  For he has not spurned or disdained
  the misery of this poor wretch,
  Did not turn away from me,
  but heard me when I cried out.
  I will offer praise in the great assembly;
  my vows I will fulfill before those who fear him.
  The poor will eat their fill;
  those who seek the LORD will offer praise.
  May your hearts enjoy life forever!"

As it turns out, this particular psalm sums up wonderfully what actually transpires between the Son and the Father. It is not a song of defeat, but a song of victory, a total reversal of what had appeared to happen.

The first words of the psalm emphasize exactly how deeply Christ had to go, in order to bring about the reconciliation of all humanity to the Father. The essence of things on the cross is actually about Jesus' commitment to obedience, done at a level never before or never since matched. It was an obedience done in absolute darkness. This was at a level united in both humanity and divinity, without a glimmer of hope or expectation. Absolute zero! As a result, however, it was absolute redemption!

The Flaw Within

Yet, at the same time, it was total love and obedience, done in a climate of total poverty and humility! To go further, this was an obedience, of which humanity was incapable from the time of Adam. No one, of themselves, beyond Jesus Christ, was capable of this kind of obedience, from the time of Abraham.

Even now, everyone ultimately fails in a yes to God. No one rises to that level by themselves. Not one of us could endure that kind of abandonment, that level of forsakenness — and still hold on to such love and obedience. Yet our Redeemer did.

I wonder if the last line of the Lords Prayer, "Deliver us from evil," might be talking about the trial that Jesus endured. Perhaps we are asking the Lord to keep us from the impossible situation that Christ alone had to endure.

This moment of Christ on the cross tells us a great deal about our inherent weaknesses, our ultimate failure to lift ourselves from the quagmire of our own failed humanity. No wonder we react so to those words of Christ on the cross, "My God, my God, why have you abandoned me?" Of its very essence, humanity since Adam is a trap of self inflicted failure. Humanity was nailed into a contradiction of nature from which there was no deliverance, save that of the love and obedience of Jesus on the cross. Clearly, we are devoid of the power to endure such.

Whenever we think we can master our existence by ourselves, we are destined for failure. Whenever we end up saying, "it's ok, I've got this," we are in trouble. We manifest the intrinsic failure built into humanity again and again, this consequence of the fall and original sin. It is not that we don't try, clearly we do, but in the long run, our efforts betray us. We are like someone jumping an abyss and falling short by inches. Despite our best efforts, the hold on the other side slips away from our grasp. We simply lose our grip.

Alternatives to Grace

By ourselves, we are willing to try anything. First there is the effort to bargain with God. That was the way of sacrifice in the temple. If I just make this sacrifice, I will buy a slot into redemption, and maybe prove myself worthy of it. Perhaps even as the Aztecs did, a human sacrifice might especially have been enough.

Then there is the form of law. If I just keep all the rules perfectly I will be acceptable, and I'll have it made with God. Maybe if I keep the law perfectly, I'll have a slot in God's plan.

But then, there is always a kind of distortion that occurs. The external nature of law has a hidden flaw within. That flaw is regarding all that cannot be written into the law, of what you cannot codify. In the end, justice and righteousness can often seem a fugitive within the boundaries of the law. In the end, thinking that salvation can come through our self investment in law alone ends up, at best, delusional.

Then, maybe magic might help. we think. If I can just get a grip on all that is behind the scenes, doing all I can do to guarantee my future, buying some security. Maybe a seance, or tarot cards, even maybe the ouija board could do it for me? Maybe this way, I can find out how to avoid any coming trial or evil, or can masquerade any intrinsic flaws I just don't know how to avoid. Again, failure!

The Surrender to Fallen Nature

In each of the above, humanity never overcomes the intrinsic flaws of human nature. All through history, we did not know what to do about those flaws, and have tried various ways to overcome them. Sometimes we tried denial or were delusional about the sinfulness of humanity. There was just no solution to this ancient weakness of human nature.

But now, there is the way of this 21st Century. If we can't fix ourselves, let's just forget about any attempt at it. After all, we have all this wealth, all this technology and science. Why do we even have to examine ourselves, and look at any inherent flaws of our humanity? Maybe, just maybe, we can make it on our own We will just redesign ourselves alone, as if we can be anything we want.

At least, thinking like this culture, maybe we might have enough that we can forget about all those weaknesses and pieces that don't really dovetail with what we imagine ourselves to be. Granted that there are wars and poverty around the world, but if we can keep it away from here, we really don't need to deal with the unsolvable flaws of human nature, we can just ignore them. Maybe we can just live without the grace from above. Finally, if we can have enough wealth, then, we don't even have to care about any problems in this culture. So much then for human nature!

Ultimate Denial or Acceptance

Fallen humanity is the colossal denial of the 21st Century. This ubiquitous denial is what makes the secular world so different in scope from previous ones. Rather than face our nature, the postmodern world has created a redefined nature where all is allowed, and everything else is forgotten, presumed to be old fashioned, superstitious or illusionary.

This is the ultimate pretense of our times. Scrubbed of any reference to God or Christ, to the flaws of being created beings, humanity now is its own creation, unaccountable to anyone or to any truth about our nature and our flaws. In the end, there is no God, no Christ who is to come, with no flaw to human nature, no purpose, mystery, or meaning to this world. There is no destiny, no origin, no explanation, no original sin, with no grace or salvation needed. What a barren wasteland!

Then there is the way of Jesus, total fidelity and obedience in the face of total darkness. Yet, even in his absolute emptiness on the cross, Christ was filled with love, to the extent of which no one else has ever been. The extent of his obedience was so universal, so total that, for once in all creation, there was an obedience to God that was total and complete. This was so much so that it was the one sufficient instance of obedience, whereby the Father could look beyond all the disobedience of his creation. The Father could recognize that this one instance of obedience so real and so complete that it could cover for all of humanity, from beginning to end. The proof was that this obedience occurred in what appeared to be the total abandonment of the cross.

Emptied for the Sake of Love

In the midst of that experience of abandonment, Christ was filled with an absolute love, a love beyond any love ever manifested in this world. This love reached to all of history, to all of creation. This love extended from the weakest of humanity to the most perverse of humanity. Thus, being totally empty in his act of obedience, Christ was at the same time filled with so much love for the Father and for us that this love still ripples around the world.

Christ's love coupled to the Father's love results in a kind of tsunami of the Holy Spirit. No wonder we are able to be counted as children of God, as disciples of Christ, as temples of the Holy Spirit. This story of abandonment and total love, then, is the source of all the grace that floods over the children of God.

This exchange between the Son and the Father then clarifies our understanding of much of the mystery of how we are redeemed, about our part in all of our salvation. The minimum on our part is that we be united as best we can to the person of Jesus Christ, alive and present to us. If we belong to Christ, even with all of our human weakness and our failings due to sin, we are then united with the one abandoned on the cross. We are then united with the one giving Himself in absolute total love. Christ chose to be united to the Father in this one act of total love and obedience. This oneness with Christ is sufficient to yield total hope for our salvation. In effect, then, we just grab the shirttails of Christ and hold on!

How do we hold on? We do so with the presence of Christ manifested to us in the Eucharist, in the Mass. There, in Communion, our connection to Christ is deepened over and over again.

We hear Him in the Gospel. We listen to the words of the Old Testament, about how he was to come. We then grasp what the first disciples heard in the Epistles and writings of the New Testament. We are transformed in the middle of a praying community to be open to Christ with us, each and every liturgy we celebrate.

Between those liturgies, we hold our hearts open to this sacred presence of Christ, risen and alive, through prayer and adoration. We keep Christ with us throughout our work week, and at home with us wherever we are.

We turn to Christ in our weakness and failure in the Sacrament of Confession. We reach out to those around us, able to discern within our neighbors that Christ is alive within them. Jesus' love and obedience wraps us into his very heart.

All of the above is to maintain our union with Christ, to live in Christ. Nothing short of that will lead to our salvation. Nothing less than that will be enough in this 21st Century, in this inverted alternative universe of Satan.

In Christ, we are held as if in a sacred kind of bubble, while all else swirls around us in a kind of chaos. In all of this, we have at the center the abandonment of Christ on the cross saturated in his love and obedience. In that cross he wraps all of us in Him, offering us to the Father in that act of absolute obedience. The door has been opened, the passageway revealed, and the hope restored for all of humanity.

Each person in humanity that chooses to belong to Christ in this world stands at the threshold of the open door, the gateway of grace.

- For the love of Christ impels us, once we have come to the conviction that one died for all; therefore, all have died. He indeed died for all, so that those who live might no longer live for themselves but for him who for their sake died and was raised. 2 Cor. 5.14-15

23. A Spiritual Epidemic

- Whoever believes in him will not be condemned, but whoever does not believe has already been condemned, because he has not believed in the name of the only Son of God. And this is the verdict, that the light came into the world, but people preferred darkness to light, because their works were evil. For everyone who does wicked things hates the light and does not come toward the light, so that his works might not be exposed. But whoever lives the truth comes to the light, so that his works may be clearly seen as done in God. (John 3:18-21)

Childhood Memories

In one of my experiences as a 11 year old, somewhere in the 1950's, there was a polio epidemic that summer. To make matters worse, my childhood was in Rochester, Minnesota, the home of the Mayo Clinic. Their major hospital, Saint Mary's, was the location where acute cases of polio were brought from all over the upper Midwest.

Rumors spread throughout the community that there were so many cases of polio in Rochester that the corridors of Saint Marys Hospital had to be utilized to house the cases that seemed to outnumber the rooms available for treatment.

I now doubt that it was of such proportions. However, in our fear and imaginations it seemed a disease of such proportions in everyone's minds. The rumors had simply taken over.

A Coincidence

To make matters worse, as an eleven year old, that summer I got sick from something, and I and my parents were terrified that it might be that dreaded disease that was thought to be so prevalent at that time, the 1950's.

In those days, a young, local doctor, named Dr. Wente, would still make house calls, and he did that for me, as a kid. After he had cleared away the question of polio for me, he visited for a few moments with my parents about one of the priests of our diocese whom he had just diagnosed with polio, Fr. Herman Berrum, a young priest well known in the Catholic community of the 1950's.

He was then a pastor just outside of Rochester, and he never walked again, except in great difficulty with crutches and leg braces, being confined mostly to a wheelchair.

My Good Fortune

Curiously, my path crossed Fr. Berrum's again, as
he took up residence at the seminary that I was
attending for college. While a student there, I
came to work with him, helping him with keeping
financial records for the seminary. Thanks to that,
he became my spiritual director, and assisted me
at that time with some very difficult questions
about the priesthood in my sophomore year in college. At that time, I did not think that I could sur-
vive any more in the seminary.

Thanks to him especially, I was able to endure to
become a priest. I am forever grateful to him, and
have long been aware of the strangest contradiction, of my coming to be helped by him, as a consequence of that apparent epidemic of polio. If it
hadn't been for that disease in his life, I don't
know how I would have overcome all my doubts
at that time in the seminary. He was the right person at the right time!

That disease of polio has long been eradicated
within this culture. Thanks to knowing Fr.
Berrum, I had come to know someone who had
dealt with the consequences of what had seemed
like a huge epidemic of the time of my youth. I
will never forget how frightening it was as an
eleven year old to have been so close to such a
mysterious disease. No one then understood how
to prevent it, or knew from where it came, or even

how to begin to prevent it. Dr. Sabin had not yet found a way to prevent that disease.

The Analogy Here

This memory has long been a kind of analogy for me, as I try to understand this strange culture of the 21st Century. I sense another epidemic, an analogous one in the midst of which we are living today. This time there is an epidemic of spiritual blindness.

This blindness appears unable to recognize the gift of grace offered to us. As a result, it is a kind of blindness that cannot recognize the gift of grace offered us in the cross of Christ. This spiritual blindness, in the culture in which we live, is one that is especially pronounced. At present it is, quite honestly, now at epic proportions. The denial today, the repression of anything spiritual today seems to grow more and more serious today. Welcome to the last days!

Often today, deeply, we worry in the same way we worried about polio, except this time it seems as if our faith could be destroyed by the secularism of this era. Thoughtful Catholics are especially on guard today.

There is a kind of spiritual blindness that almost appears contagious today. The media is fond of reinforcing such an illusion. The message today is that there is no Christ. Further it is assumed that the Church is a headless cadaver, a sinful failure incapable of accommodating the wondrous secularism of this Century. This situation is the context of a new and pervasive spiritual blindness.

This spiritual blindness has always been a part of our humanity, from the time of Adam and Eve. This disease of the soul revolves around an ability we have acquired as fallen creatures. This ability inherent in us is to see darkness as if it were light.

Furthermore, this particular form of blindness is to be convinced deeply that the truth is somehow a falsehood. This malady is something that we can convince ourselves of, in order to possess whatever it is that we want.

Spiritual blindness inverts the light into darkness, and provides us with an alternative reality that exists only in our minds, unconnected to anything. This blindness centers exactly around the inability to recognize the love of God Our Father, in sending his Son, Jesus Christ.

This form of blindness hides the total, spectacular sacrifice of his Son on the cross, specifically for our salvation. Spiritual blindness easily becomes a way of living a lie. It makes us fixtures in the inverted alternative universe of Satan.

The Consequences in our Times

In our contemporary situation the media seems lost in that blindness, looking at the Catholic Church as some sort of human institution, led by bishops and priests they think misguided. They look at our moral stances as a form of bigotry, wondering how any group in so modern of a world could possibly hold to so many things no longer valued by society. Our faith supposedly has so many teachings assumed out of line today, that we are bigoted about sex, purity, chastity, marriage, and children, to name just a few.

Today, education bypasses any and all of Catholic teachings. Sociology has long since abandoned any of our values. Psychology is believed able to fix anything, religion being unnecessary. Science views us as a kind of mystical enchantment, approximately at the same level as pagan mythology, a realm of fairies and unicorns. They all wonder how we could hold on to something so far from the truth, us being lost in darkness in this new world of enlightenment. All of them see the Church as this headless cadaver, an inert remnant of bygone days.

None of them sense that the head and core of the Church is in Jesus Christ Himself, forcefully present here and now. The Eucharist appears to them as an astounding piece of misbelief.

The Man Born Blind

There is a passage in John's Gospel that high-lights this inversion. There was a miracle of a man born blind, where Jesus restored his ability to see. The man is questioned repeatedly by the pharisees about how this happened, and they even called in his parents to testify. Eventually, the pharisees throw the man out, in absolute denial of the miracle.

Later Jesus finds him again, with the pharisees still around.

- Jesus said, "I came into this world for judgment, so that those who do not see might see, and those who do see might become blind."
  Some of the Pharisees who were with him heard this and said to him, "Surely we are not also blind, are we?"
  Jesus said to them, "If you were blind, you would have no sin; but now you are saying, 'We see,' so your sin remains."
  (John 9:40-41)

This disease of spiritual blindness, the inability to recognize the overwhelming gift of grace, has grown to immense, epidemic proportions in in these postmodern times. Spiritual blindness is now such that few now understand how to prevent it, or know from where it came, or even what it is.

It is not even perceived as a blindness. Instead, the assumption is that anyone of faith is the one blind in these days. This kind of blindness today saturates the spiritual climate of our times, so much so, that it could be referred to as a kind of epidemic of spiritual blindness unique to our times. The root of this spiritual blindness is the attempt to build a world view that has no God within it, no grace, no divine love, with nothing transcendent about it.

In essence, without our Father in heaven, or without his Divine Son, everything falls into a kind of darkness, mistaken for light.

All this has made the gift of grace invisible to our postmodern world. This invisibility of grace is an incredible loss to the world today. Only with an awareness of grace do we have the power to confront the darkness, masquerading as light.

This supposed absence of grace is the one key piece without which there can be no true light. Without grace there can be no true power to address this era, no way to complete our fragmented and flawed human nature. Gracelessness is the tragedy of the 21st Century.

From Where Have We Come?

Thus the central question is always about the mystery of where we come from. Without Our Father in heaven, and without the saving Grace of Jesus Christ, giving Himself on our behalf in the cross, there is simply a void, a darkness. No matter how this world tries, this void is simply an emptiness of meaning, a wilderness of hope, and a shipwreck of morality. No wonder we can recognize the epidemic of darkness and spiritual blindness today for exactly what it is.

Our Father and His Son, Jesus Christ, has been deleted from the postmodern consciousness. In that deletion lies a darkness from which there is no escape.

One of the characteristics of an epidemic is that it has a tendency to spread like wildfire, seemingly without any limitation, lacking any source to which we can attribute its rise. This is also the case within our postmodern world. Spiritual blindness spreads is a similar way, affecting far more than those who have committed themselves to it. There are many victims of this secularism, innocents swept away in all these delusions of darkness. Even we ourselves, as Catholic, are tempted by the darkness.

The True Light

One might think that this epidemic of our times should be a moment of great discouragement of the disciples of Christ. On the contrary, our times can be an era of great evangelization. In reality, there is nothing out there except the true light. Once someone awakens to the delusions and falsehoods of the postmodern world, there will be only one place to turn, only one to whom to turn.

I believe that Christ will be incredibly active in the generation ahead, stunningly visible to any and all who can no longer fathom this age, and will turn in humility and desperation towards Christ. Once that person turns, only Christ will satisfy what they are seeking. Only the true light will be sufficient for them, surrounded as it is by the love of God, the grace that flows from the Holy Spirit.

The foundation stone, then, of recovery from this epidemic of darkness is to acknowledge the presence of Jesus Christ, alive in our midst and in our hearts. When we are open to His presence, He will make that awakening happen. This simple, humble step awakens within us the light of Christ, allowing us to recognize the darkness for what it is. This awakening is nothing complicated, nothing beyond being open to Christ. Most often, we don't even have to find Christ, He will find us. Indeed, this is exactly what will be able to occur, even in this epidemic of darkness. The simplicity of light is astounding, and open to all who would so choose.

What Falls into Place in Christ

Immediately, upon the acceptance of Christ, two things fall into place, in the new light within us.

The first of these is a changed awareness of our sinfulness. We are awakened often times with a new sense of the harm and the loss that our sins have done to those we love, and to the life we had been leading. Strangely, this awareness of our sins does not cause us to withdraw from Christ, but rather to pursue Him more ardently. For the first time we can see, there is light, and we can acknowledge now, what before we fought so ferociously to deny.

Our sins at first seem like the monstrous shadows, shadows much bigger than the extent of our sins. However, with the light of Christ shining on our sins, those shadows suddenly appear smaller, something that we can face. Christ makes those shadows shrink.

Somehow, our sins, once acknowledged, bring us closer and closer to Christ. This is one of the miracles of coming into the light, despite what the light reveals to us about ourselves. Christ makes it safe to acknowledge we are sinners. That we are sinners is not the end, it is the beginning of the light.

The second part of coming to the light is that, despite our sins, we find that there is a goodness in us for which we cannot account. In this goodness, unearned and unmerited, we discover and acknowledge that God Himself has placed that within us. This sense of goodness is simply revealed to us by the grace from above.

This new awareness is the astounding impact of the gift of grace. For the most part, we become stunned by what the Father has done in sending his Son, and what the Son has done in the moment of the exchange on the cross. All that, despite our sinfulness! In the cross we discover a new, deep seated sense of who and what we are, precious somehow in the eyes of Christ. This is what can only be summarized by the one word, grace.

What Grace Reveals

In addition we uncover an identity, framed and focused by the love of God. This new awareness changes how we live, and colors what we do with our lives. Even more, we see a destiny and a meaning to our lives that we could never have found by ourselves. Now even our suffering and our losses take on value. Thanks to the gift of grace within us, everything in our lives now completes us, transforms us, and remakes us in Christ.

We continuously celebrate that newness that we have found, by turning our hearts to Christ. This happens most centrally in the Eucharist. In every Mass we are brought to that sacred moment on the cross when Christ offers us up to his Father in heaven, and the Father accepts us along with his Son. We then kneel there, witnesses to the moment of our salvation revealed to us.

This moment is sealed in our Communion, where each time in that reception, we are taken back to the instant when we discovered the light. We now look, from Christ's perspective, at our sinfulness, and rejoice in who and what we have become in Christ. We then can witness that there is a healing that reshapes us into the image of Christ, lifting us out of the darkness of these times, enriching us beyond anything we could have imagined. We awaken to the grace that flows from above us, breathless that the Lord above would do such a thing for us.

24. Hope

- And the Word became flesh and made his
  dwelling among us and we saw his glory,
  the glory as of the Father's only Son, full
  of grace and truth.
  John testified to him and cried out, saying,
  "This was he of whom I said, 'The one who
  is coming after me ranks ahead of me because he existed before me.'" From his fullness we have all received, grace in place of
  grace, because while the law was given
  through Moses, grace and truth came
  through Jesus Christ.
  John 1:14-17

False Hope Today

To be Catholic in this era of the secular requires a
knowledge of especially one thing. What we especially need to know is the theological gift of hope.
We need to understand this gift of hope in a total
and complete way.

The secular era alway mimics the qualities that
the Catholic of these postmodern times requires.
In fact, it is the very essence of the antichrist to
mimic virtually everything that we hold precious

as Catholics. Thus, there is a false form of hope that mimics true theological hope.

This false sense of hope is the result of the presence of the antichrist. This false hope is attempt to camouflage the distortion and inversion of Satan's universe, as if proposing a simpler and easier way than that of the Gospel. Hope itself is a primary target of the antichrist.

This false hope, suggested by Satan, is a kind of horizontal hope, an achievable hope by our own power to grasp the future, to build in guarantees for the days ahead. This false hope says "Look at what we have done all on our own!" This kind of horizontal hope is built upon the belief, ungrounded in reality, that things will continue to get better and better, that more and more will be allowed to us in the future.

Curiously, the past is always condemned as being inadequate and limited in its makeup. The past is assumed to be superstitious, mythical, and illusionary, as compared to the certainty of the present and the future. In fact, the future is presented to us as virtually guaranteed to be better than the past or the present. All the advancement of the past fifty or so years is just the beginning of an even better times ahead.

Tearing up Track to Lay Ahead

Once I saw a film, as a kid, a western about the building of the transcontinental railroad. The key point of the film was that the connection between the Eastern and the Western portions of the transcontinental railroad had to be made by such and such a date. However, on the Eastern portion they had run out of track and tie, and thus were unable to complete their contract.

Then, the characters in the film struck an ingenious method for the first Eastern train to meet the one from the West on time. They simply tore up the track and tie behind the train, and relaid it in front of the engine repeatedly, thus allowing the train to arrive on time. In the process, they had destroyed what was behind them, in order to achieve the illusion of completion.

How similar to these times, deflating the past on a promise of the future, tearing up what has been given to the present on the hope of something yet to come. Our postmodern world has ripped up centuries of faith and truth in order to shape a future of merely human dimensions, godless and without any transcendental character.

This promise seems to assume a future of even more wealth, even better technology, that we will live longer and more fulfilled lives, and that death will continue to recede. All this is without reference to such things as climate change, the increase of addictions, the massacres happening in our culture, or the continuing growth of suicides. This promise of horizontal hope is illusionary to the max. That's the very essence of horizontal hope.

In addition, in this kind of horizontal hope, we get to take credit for its existence. In brief, we will have created a kind of hope on our own. We are the originators, the source of this hope. It is as if we never ever needed a Father in heaven, a Redeemer of the world, or a Spirit to shower us with grace. We did it ourselves, and look at the success we are having!

Hope from Above

How different theological hope is. Theological hope is vertical, descending upon us from above. This kind of hope takes the sin and failure, the violence and disfunction in our times and makes them the instrument of grace, bringing goodness out of the evil, and truth out of the lies. This hope augurs the inexplicable and exponential birth of the final days of the Kingdom of God in our midst.

There is a certainty in theological hope, one not present in horizontal hope. This certainty is not based on ourselves. There's no lifting ourselves by the bootstraps. Indeed, we are still sinners, even as disciples of Christ. We have no guarantees on our own. We do not expect our God to just overlook our failures, and then give us credit for how hard we tried. Ours in not a hope of desperation, hoping to snag the bottom rung of the ladder of purgatory somehow. None of that fits here.

The essence of our hope, our theological hope, is firmly based on what comes to us from revelation, truths so powerful from above that their knowledge overrides all our fear and trembling about the present or the future. Theological hope is surely one of the greatest signs of the presence of grace with us. This grace has the power to overwhelm whatever signs of failure and inadequacy Satan can instill within these times.

True hope and grace are virtual twins in our faith life. They feed each other. The greater the grace, the more the hope. Where this kind of hope is present, there is an overwhelming sense of God's grace with us.

The Anchor of Hope from Above

These truths shower us with truths that we would not know on our own, that we could not grasp by ourselves. These truths are the fallout of the gift of grace in our midst. In addition, these truths are astounding in such a way that they are more than we can ever get our arms around completely. We are left standing, wondering in human terms, "Could this possibly be true?" Yet, we know it to be so!

This source of our theological hope is above and beyond us, again and again. This hope telegraphs a truth beyond anything that we could have conjured up, or that we could have imagined. This anchor of our hope is unlike a ship's anchor that reaches downward to grab ahold of something below. The anchor of our Christian hope is grounded in the cross of Jesus, attached to the Holy Spirit, secure in the kingdom of God. This hope is anchored from above.

Yet, the facts are so simple about our hope. Perhaps that is what makes them so astounding. The fact is that Our Father in heaven has a kind of love for us that has no limit. Our Father in heaven, keenly aware of the damage that resides in us from the time of Adam and Eve, seemed to have a plan from all eternity to send his Son to us, putting everything in His hands. This was an incredibly radical solution to our broken and fragmented humanity. All this comes, in spite of our sinfulness.

His Son came to give his life, heart and soul, for our salvation. That act, on the cross, was so extensive, so deep that all of humanity would then have an open door back to the salvation so squandered by us and our initial parents. This meant a solution for all humanity from the beginning of time to the end of time. This act by Christ on the cross cements the pathway back to the Father.

Not only that, but we as Catholics, in our celebration of the Mass extended from the moment of the last supper, experience this very moment of our redemption again and again. In the Mass we have the very moment of Christ's victory on the cross. Every time we celebrate the Eucharist that is so. We are there with Christ at that sacred moment, in that immense exchange between the Son and the Father. In that moment we celebrate that instant of total reversal of our future. We end up as witnesses to the moment of our own salvation, watching ourselves being lifted up in Christ as an offering to the Father. We see the Father consecrating the sacrifice of his Son, raising Him from the dead. Theological hope has less to do with our actions or efforts, but has everything to do with what Christ has done and continues to do within us.

The Signs We Have in Hope

No wonder that we can recognize the absolute heart of our hope, and that we can have that hope with us throughout whatever struggles we have with our nature and with this secular era. This is a kind of resource of hope that cannot fail us, that won't abandon us ever.

The signs we look for in our theological hope are not material, acquired possessions of the things of this world. No, the signs we possess are ones that have come to us from above, tremendous signs of divine love, of a grace that reaches to the very marrow of our souls. How different this hope from that of our contemporary secular world!

Again and again, we get to watch the minuscule start of a piece of the kingdom of God, fostered and empowered by the love of the Holy Spirit. We see everything that is touched by the grace that takes this world from nothingness to exponential growth into this Kingdom of God. The greater the nothingness around us, the greater the grace and growth of the Kingdom of God in our hearts and faith life. We know from what happened on the cross, and from what we experience in the Eucharist, that we have an indelible source of hope. In the expectation that we have from above, the hope that we have will never ever not be present to us!

Even the immensity of failure and collapse of this 21st Century points us to this theological hope, that everything about these times will instruct us in the kind of hope that will not fail us, that will not lead us to horizontal expectations that are the lie of the antichrist. True hope will highlight all the illusions of the inverted alternative universe of Satan.

Whenever we start to have doubts, we need to return to the cross, and to the Eucharist, where we can find the true source of hope, even in this inverted alternative universe of Satan. The truth of revelation is undeniable even in this era, and becomes all the stronger amid the chaos and deception that we find in these times.

Peace and Order

The touchstone of hope is a sense of peace, a kind of theological peace. This peace can exist in the midst of chaos. This is the inward experience of true hope. Peace derives only from the hope that comes from above. In the gift of grace from above arises the hope that telegraphs this sense of true peace in our hearts.

So it is, in all the connection with Christ, that we become possessors of inner peace, the kind that only Christ's presence can give.

Also, only in Christ do we take on a meaning and purpose in our lives that is greater than ourselves, such a meaning or purpose that even our failures and personal struggles come to fruition in Christ.

Last of all, instead of the chaos and disfunction of the secular world, to be connected to Christ gives us a kind of order in our lives, whereby we can live day by day in union with Christ. Christ gives us an inward structure to our lives. Christ orders our lives in our weakness and sinfulness, giving us access to what is supernatural within us. To live in Christ gives that spirit of our life that the Father has intended for us from all creation. Christ, and the grace that comes from Him, gives us the ability to start over, to begin anew, turning our backs on the sinfulness of our past. This order in our hearts stems directly from the gift of true hope.

This connection is absolutely vital for the Catholic in this day and age. It begins with the yes to Christ, and grows from there. Apart from that connection to Christ, we can do nothing. In each of us, when we are connected to Christ, we cherish the gift of the Mass and the Eucharist, as that keeps us connected, and strengthens us day by day for whatever challenges this postmodern world will have for us. Thus grace and hope, peace and order form the web of protection that surrounds us especially in this realm of the twenty-first Century.

The Silver Thread

For us who are disciples of Christ, God's grace is an unbreakable silver thread that comes from above. We have no power to grasp it on our own, but only the power to be connected to Jesus Christ, allowing Him to heal and transform us into disciples. That connection opens up for us the presence of the Holy Spirit, who rains down the gift of grace into to our souls, and joins us to the kingdom of God. In that Spirit our flawed and broken humanity is lifted up to live beyond our natures, within the stunning and healing grace that we could never have accessed on our own.

With Christ, everything from above flows downward and inward. What an astounding miracle this inward change to us is in Christ, this flow of divine grace into our souls, manifested with a sense of hope, pointed to a spiritual peace and order that is thoroughly contrary to the times in which we live.